About Lake Allen

Born in Portsmouth in 1799, Lake Allen was from early on a keen historian and Classicist. The son of a hatmaker whose shop was on Portsmouth High Street, he was looked after by his grandfather, Lake Taswell.

The older man instilled in the boy a love of history, and by 16, he was writing articles about Portsmouth's past. A keen researcher, he scoured ancient documents and histories to produce at the tender age of 18 his *History of Portsmouth*.

The founder of Portsmouth's first debating society, *The Athenæum*, he was good friends with Frederick Madden, who went on to become curator of the British Museum's manuscripts.

Lake Allen died in 1824 aged just 25 years old, leaving this book as his lasting legacy.

About the editor

Matt Wingett was born in Portsmouth and has a fascination with the city.

He is a writer of fiction, history and tv drama. He has written several fiction stories based around Portsmouth, a study of Sir Arthur Conan Doyle's spiritualism and has written episodes of ITV's *The Bill* as well as stage plays.

Also by Matt Wingett

Fiction:

The Tourist
The Boiler Pool
The Tube Healer
Turn The Tides Gently
The Song of Miss Tolstoy

Non-Fiction:

Conan Doyle and the Mysterious World of Light

Contributor to:

Portsmouth Fairy Tales for Grown-Ups

Editor:

Ten Years In A Portsmouth Slum, by Robert Dolling
The History of Portsmouth, by Lake Allen

THE HISTORY
OF
PORTSMOUTH

THE HISTORY
OF
PORTSMOUTH

by

LAKE ALLEN

Edited by

MATT WINGETT

Life Is Amazing
Heritage Series

A Life Is Amazing Paperback
The History of Portsmouth
First published in this edition 2015 by Life Is Amazing
ISBN: 978-0-9572413-6-7
First Thus Edition

CONTENTS

Editor's Introduction

Lake Allen was born in Portsmouth in 1799, the son of Herbert Allen, a hatter based in the High Street and Mary, daughter of Lake Taswell, a landowner and co-proprietor of the Portsmouth Theatre. Considering Mary to have married beneath her station, Taswell banished her from his house; but when he saw that his newly arrived grandson was sickly and often in need of medical attention, Taswell relented and offered him a home under his roof.

In 1775, Taswell had written a 52 page tourist booklet, *A Portsmouth Guide,* which he retitled *The New Portsmouth Guide* in the revised 1790 edition. This was very likely the inspiration for *The History of Portsmouth*, while the love of study and scholarship Taswell instilled in his grandson gave him the tools to realise it.

As young as 16, Allen was writing articles on Portsmouth history. At 18, he produced his only book, the sometimes brilliant, occasionally eccentric, and deeply ambitious *History of Portsmouth*.

Its scope is impressive. Starting with the 501 AD battle recorded in the *Anglo Saxon Chronicles*, the book uncovers numerous obscure facts about ancient Portsmouth. Allen's copious footnotes reveal that he researched assiduously – quoting not only the great historians of his period, but numerous ancient documents. A keen Classicist, he translated mediæval Latin texts, and also filled in details of Portsmouth life with first-hand impressions.

Flashes of affection for his home town occur throughout his book.

He has a Romantic sensibility, revelling in reports of ruins and ancient battles, even quoting popular poets as he eulogises the health-promoting benefits of the sea air and of bathing.

Each chapter adopts a theme. The first deals with the town's ancient history, for which documentation was sparse. The information Allen unearths is often confined to troop movements or the departure of kings overseas; but there are also wonderful details in the footnotes.

Tangential facts abound, for example, the inventory of riches held in St Thomas's church (now Portsmouth Cathedral), or the quantity of wine imported through different ports in the Middle Ages. Sometimes he repeats himself, as he does in mention of Leland's description of the town.

At times, Lake Allen seems to want to impetuously rush at the reader with a novel fact, saying, "Hey! Look at this!" At other times, his writing shows real maturity. His account of John Felton's psychological motivations for his assassination of the Duke Of Buckingham is masterful. In a few short sentences he lays down the character, the motives and the events leading to the murder. Later, his mention that, till only a few years before, the gibbet on which Felton's body was hung could could still be seen on Southsea beach, directly engages the reader with an infamous moment in history.

This, then, is Allen's method. He finds relics of the past which connect us with people and stories of long ago. Allen often refers to Portsmouth as "here", "this place", rather than taking the more objective choice of "the town" or "Portsmouth", bringing the reader with him through its streets, to stand by the quay, marvel at the dockyard or peer down from a castle's ramparts.

At times, he is inadvertently comic. Writing about the way the boundaries of Portsmouth were marked, he paints a picture of the

Mayor accompanied by his Serjeant-at-Mace and various dignitaries in all their finery, rowing around the island accompanied by a boatload of musicians, performing antiquated ceremonies. At another point, a procession of dignitaries marking boundaries on land where the buildings have changed are forced to put somebody "over the wall" to ensure they follow the ancient route; or march through the middle of someone's house in accordance with tradition.

The chapter on the Borough of Portsmouth gives insights into political battles, such as the dissent of *Patriotic* elements in the council who oppose the Government's commitment to the American War. In retaliation, the Government dismisses all but the two lifelong Patriot council members. The Patriots retaliate by obtaining a judgement to likewise dismiss all but the two lifelong pro-Government councillors. The Borough remains thus, in deadlock, for nine years. Other examples of systemic corruption, such as the election of a five-year-old to the office of Burgess in order to boost numbers, remind us that politicians seeking unscrupulously to grasp power is the rule of all ages.

Other chapters describe the town of Portsmouth, Gosport, Haslar, the Isle of Wight and other areas, giving an insight into the composition of the town and its environs, along with customs and features that would otherwise long have been lost in obscurity. For example, the giant bellows in the dockyard that required a suspended man to work them, or the Armoury at the end of St. Mary's Street (near the site of modern Armoury Lane), which contained a horde of antique weapons in impressive display.

Other events, such as the massive explosion that blew open Southsea Castle or the sinking of the *Royal George* are reported, as are the massive fires that swept through the dockyard in the mid-Eighteenth Century, and the visit to the town by Emperors and Kings who were allies in the Napoleonic wars. With such events, Allen seeks to remind us that Portsmouth is nationally important, and has been for centuries.

There are also times when he finds the limits of his knowledge. His account of the geological origins of Portsea Island shows him overreaching himself:

> PORTSMOUTH is situated on the Island of Portsea, which is about sixteen miles in circumference. This part of the country lies low, and appears to have been gradually gained from the sea, or from the effect of some extraordinary convulsion of nature that might have probably at the same time separated the Isle of Wight from the main land of Hampshire.

The phrase "might have probably" reminds us that this is the work of an 18-year-old who had applied himself diligently to his subject to the best of his powers.

Whilst his ignorance of Portsmouth's geology is apparent, so is his enthusiasm for the town. We variously find that the air and water are uniquely suited for sea bathing (a newly fashionable pastime which led to the founding of the Victorian resort of Southsea), that the markets are excellent, that the sand is perfect for the bather (would *that* were still true!), that leisure sailors splashed by the Solent off of Southsea do not catch cold, and even that Portsmouth broccoli is the best in the kingdom.

Furthermore, considering the modernday rivalry between Portsmouth and Southampton, it is amusing to read his comments asserting the inferiority of the rival resort.

The book was well received in Portsmouth and brought Allen a degree of local renown that drew others to him. He befriended a younger boy, Frederick Madden, and together they co-founded Portsmouth's first literary and philosophical debating society, *The Athenæum*.

The venture was short-lived, with Madden and Allen soon falling out. But the calibre of these two minds that met in Portsmouth is perhaps evinced by the fact that Madden went on to become the curator of manuscripts at the British Museum and later received a knighthood for his work.

Lake Allen had always been sickly, and he died in 1824 at the tender age of 25. Sir Frederick Madden, who had by this time made up their friendship, mourned his passing. It is a Romantic cliché to say that Lake Allen could easily have gone on to great things and that his death was a *tragedy* (as a Classicist, Allen would have complained bitterly about the misuse of that word), but it is also most likely true.

A monument to Lake Allen and his grandfather can be found in Portsmouth Cathedral. His book is an equally fitting memorial.

Matt Wingett
Southsea, 2015.

Portsmouth In Lake Allen's Time.

The Portsmouth of Lake Allen's birth was a town encompassed by earth and stone fortifications. Defensive bastions jutted into an encircling moat, from which projected further fortifications, or ravelins. The town itself had a predominantly army presence, with soldiers garrisoned here to man the defences.

Along the tops of the walls, ancient elm trees spread their branches, which some claimed would lessen the impact of shot fired from enemy ships. Not far from the Square Tower, blocking Broad Street, stood the King James Gate (pictured on the cover of this book). On its far side was a moat and drawbridge, making *Spice Island* a genuine island.

In 1812, the government began the process of buying land along the dockyard's boundaries to strengthen its fortifications. Plans were drawn up to build extra barracks at the north of Portsea Island to further protect Portsbridge, the only road on and off of the island, already protected by the first phase of the Hilsea Lines. All this preparation came against the backdrop of the Napoleonic Wars, in which Portsmouth, as Britain's premier naval base, was a central player.

Beyond the moat on Spice Island, all manner of debauchery could be encountered in its pubs and drinking dens, where it wasn't unknown for a sailor to blow a year's pay in a weekend. It is possible that the young Lake Allen, walking along the ramparts, saw captured enemy ships towed past the Hot Walls into harbour, or witnessed sailors entering the King James Gate, intent on enjoying their liberty, to fight, to drink and to whore in time-honoured tradition.

In 1817, at the time Lake Allen's book was published, Portsmouth had been elevated in the national consciousness. Aware of the martial history of the town, Lake was clearly proud of the numerous visits paid by successive monarchs seeking to inspect the fleet, meet newly-arrived queens and princes or leave on foreign adventures. He writes with relish of the arrival of the Duke of Wellington and Marshall Blücher in the great celebration of 1814 that marked the supposed defeat of the French by the Allied Powers in the previous year.

The town was not completely given over to martial matters, however. Portsmouth was already beginning to form literary connections. To the north and west of Portsmouth, the newly-founded town of Portsea was growing. Just a few years earlier in 1812, Elizabeth Dickens had gone into labour at a ball in the Beneficial Society, and was rushed to the Mile End Road to give birth to future author, Charles Dickens. Jane Austen's brothers, as naval officers, were often in the town, and the writer Captain Frederick Marryat had no doubt already observed the original lady of easy virtue whom he later fictionalised accosting his naïve young officer, Peter Simple:

I had arrived opposite a place called Sally Port, when a young lady very nicely dressed, looked at me very hard and said, "Well, Reefer, how are you off for soap?" I was astonished at the question, and more so at the interest which she seemed to take in my affairs. I answered, "Thank you, I am very well off; I have four cakes of Windsor, and two bars of yellow for washing." She laughed at my reply, and asked me whether I would walk home and take a bit of dinner with her. I was astonished at this polite offer, and I said that I should be most happy. I thought I might venture to offer my arm, which she accepted, and we proceeded up High Street on our way to her home.

Peter Simple, Captain Frederick Marryat, Chapter 4.

Meanwhile, to the north east of Portsmouth, the more respectable Croxton Town was newly built. The development, which would expand and become the new town of Southsea, already offered a seaside resort, with bathing machines and picturesque views of the Isle of Wight in its favour. Much of Southsea Common was overgrown with gorse bushes and flooded, forming the Great Morass, while other parts were used for mustering troops. A gate made of whale bones opened on to Southsea Common, which some reports say was notorious for its immoral goings-on after nightfall.

Lake Allen's Portsmouth in 1817 was far different from the Portsmouth of today. Fratton was still a rural location, with Froddington Manor at its heart, Buckland was a hamlet not far from Kingston, whilst Baffins was a country estate and deer park originally given to Anne of Cleves by King Henry VIII as part of her divorce settlement.

Something of that old town can be traced in its current shape, and in names such as Ravelin Park which remind us of the fortifications Lake Allen knew so well.

It takes imagination nowadays to trace its slow development, from a few desultory fishing huts, to a town ravaged firstly by Danish marauders and then by French sailors, to finally becoming a fortified naval base on which the country relied in the Napoleonic Wars.

Lake Allen helps that imagination along.

On The Edits In This Book

When I came to prepare this new edition, I had to make several decisions on what to modernise and what to leave. In some instances, I realised the general knowledge taken for granted in Lake Allen's day is not shared by modern readers; so, I have added some translations of Latin phrases, clarifications of Roman numerals and some notes on dates of the reigns of kings. I have changed the mediæval conventions which render the last *i* in a string of numerals as *j*; for example *iij* is replaced with the more modern *iii*. Similarly, conventions that represented 96 as a Roman numeralised *four-score and sixteen* I have represented with the accepted modern method – ie: *xcvi*. My footnotes are placed in square brackets, Allen's are not.

Regarding the language, I didn't want to change its flavour, but I was also aware that one thing in particular got in the way – punctuation.

Lake Allen's punctuation was extremely precise, but very much of its time. Allen marked with a comma every clause and sub-clause, leading to a series of staccato phrases separated by commas. At times this suited well: some of his writing simply strings related ideas together, then divides them with commas. However, too often the commas impede the flow of the read. I have adjusted them accordingly.

I have retained his use of semi-colons, which he often uses with a conjunction where the modern writer would use a full-stop.

Similarly, I have kept his use of colons and his use of italics, with a few tidyings up.

I have removed many of the full-stops from abbreviations such as *Esq, Mr, N, S, E and W,* because they make sense in context, and at times they misleadingly appear to mark the end of a sentence.

Regarding spelling, I have kept the archaisms to retain the original flavour. Thus, I favoured *chuzing* over *choosing, Gibralter* over *Gibraltar,* alongside many other examples.

Direct quotes of archaic texts, such as the passage from *Leland's Itinerary* and the letters from Oliver Cromwell, I have kept inviolate, with all their chaotic, non-uniform vigour.

Where I have detected a typesetter's error, I have set it right; where I have been unsure, I have left it. Thus, I have kept the incorrect spelling *yacht* as *yatch* at one point. These variations (or mistakes) are, I feel, redolent of the epoch, when auto-correct was not even a dream.

Finally, I have left all Allen's words in order, with one exception. The author's preface has an ungainly interjection, which I have footnoted.

The rest is just as the author intended.

THE

History of Portsmouth;

CONTAINING

A FULL AND ENLARGED ACCOUNT

OF ITS

ANCIENT AND PRESENT STATE;

WITH

A PARTICULAR DESCRIPTION OF THE DOCK-YARD, GUN-WHARF,
HASLAR HOSPITAL, THE TOWNS OF PORTSEA AND
GOSPORT, PORCHESTER CASTLE.

THE

ISLE OF WIGHT,

And the most remarkable Places in the vicinity.

TO WHICH IS ADDED

AN APPENDIX,

CONTAINING MANY OF THE CHARTERS GRANTED
TO THE TOWN, &c. &c.

———

BY LAKE ALLEN.

———

"Non de Villis, domibusque alienis;
——— Sed quod magis ad nos
Pertinet, et nescire malum est, agitamus."
                                        HORACE.

LONDON:

Printed by Hatfield and Co. 20, Great New Street, Gough Square ;

AND SOLD BY

S. MILLS, HIGH-STREET, PORTSMOUTH ; T. WHITEWOOD,
QUEEN-STREET, PORTSEA ; W. JOHNSON, HIGH-STREET,
GOSPORT ; AND ALL THE NEIGHBOURING BOOKSELLERS.

—

1817.

PREFACE.

As the salubrity of the air, the moderate distance of the town from the metropolis, and the beauty of the surrounding country contribute to give Portsmouth a decided superiority over many other places in the Kingdom, it is hoped that the following work which contains a particular account of every thing worthy of observation, will not be unacceptable to the public.

The *ancient* history of this place is probably *less* known than that of any other town in the kingdom, and particular care has been taken not to insert any particulars which have not been *fully* authenticated by historians.[1]

---

1 [Here the author included the following, paragraphs, which I have removed because it interferes with the flow of ideas:]

The reader will perceive from perusing this work, that Portsmouth made no inconsiderable figure during the time of our Saxon and Norman monarchs; and that also from the importance of its maritime situation it was highly favoured by all our succeeding kings. Indeed from the singular excellence of its port it afforded the greatest convenience for the equipping of fleets, many of which were fitted out here from the earliest periods of history.

In the reign of Edward the III, this town was in a very flourishing condition; but in the year 1338, it was burnt by the French, upon which, this monarch forgave the inhabitants a debt they owed him, and remitted their fee farm rent for *ten* years, within which space they rebuilt their town, and so recovered themselves, as to be enabled to fit out a squadron which they employed against France, and thereby obtained a great booty.] - Ed.

But though neither labour nor expense has been spared to render it worthy the acceptance of the public, yet the editor does not indulge himself with the hope that it is superior to criticism, on the contrary, he submits it, with extreme diffidence to their candid and impartial perusal, and shall feel obliged to any who may suggest improvements, supply defects, or communicate corrections, to which a proper regard shall be paid should the reception of the present, encourage the publication of another edition.

L.A.

Portsmouth, June 28th, 1817.

THE
History of Portsmouth
CHAPTER I
Its Ancient History

THE very name of Portsmouth implies its situation, as it stands at
the mouth of a harbour or port. It lies in North Lat. 50°. 48', and
West Long, 1°. 1'. The earliest historical account respecting it appears
in the *Saxon Chronicle*, A.D. 501 , in which year a body of Saxons
landed at *Portesmuth* from two large gallies[2] under the command of
Porth and his two sons, *Bleda* and *Magla*, who having defeated the
Britons immediately opposed to them, and killed their commander,
took possession of the adjacent country, which Porth afterwards held
in vassalage of Cerdic.[3]

---

2 "Venerunt cum duobus navibus maximis." - HEN. HUNT.

3 Rudborne.

Mr. Turner in his history of the Anglo Saxons has made the following
remarks on the battle fought here between the Britons and Porth, the Saxon:
— "Some of the battles mentioned by the ancient Welch poets are those
between Cerdic and the Britons; one of them is the *Battle of Longborth*. In
this conflict, Arthur was the commander in chief, and Geraint ab Erbin was a
Prince of Devonshire, united with him against the Saxons. *Llywurch Hen*, in
his elegy on his friend, describes the progress of the battle. The shout of
onset, and the terrible obscurity which followed the shock, are succeeded by
the fearful incidents which alarm humanity into abhorrence of war. The
edges of the blades in contact, the gushing of blood, the weapons of the
heroes with gore fast dropping, men surrounded with terror, the crimson
gash upon the chieftain's brow, biers with the dead, a tumultuous running
together, the combatants striving with blood up to the knees and ravens

The coasts of Britain were in the year 787 very much infested by a race of ferocious and destructive rovers called *Danes*. It would fill a volume to enumerate all the descents these merciless marauders made upon these coasts for more than two centuries; if they conquered in their attacks, the depredations they committed and the carnage they made were unbounded; if they were beaten, they retired for the present, but soon returned to the assault with fresh vigour. As no part of England escaped the unwelcome visits of these pirates, there can be no doubt but Portsmouth came in for its full share of the general calamity.[4]

---

feasting on human prey, compose the dismal picture which this ancient bard has transmitted to us of a battle, in which he was personally engaged.

"The valiant *Geraint ab Erbin* was slain; the issue of the conflict is not precisely stated, but some ambiguous expressions concur with the absence of all triumphant language, to indicate that the Britons did not prevail.

"As Longborth literally signifies the haven of ships, and was some harbour on the southern coast, we may consider this poem as describing the conflict at *Portsmouth*, when *Porth* landed." Vol. I. c. ii. p. 99.

4 "The Danes (says Hume) avoided coming to a general engagement, which was not suited to their plan of operations. Their vessels were small, and ran easily up the creeks and rivers, where they drew them ashore; and having formed an entrenchment round them, which they generally guarded with part of their number, the remainder scattered themselves every where, and carrying off the inhabitants, cattle, and goods, they hastened to their ships and quickly disappeared. If the military force of the country were assembled, for there was no time for troops to march from a distance, the Danes were either able to repulse them and continue their ravages with impunity, or they betook themselves to their vessels, and setting sail, suddenly invaded some distant quarter which was not prepared for their reception. Every part of England was held in continual alarm; and the inhabitants of one county durst not give assistance to those of another, lest

A.D. 838. Ethelwulph was scarce seated on the throne, when a fleet of Danes[5] appeared between this place and Southampton; after they had roved up and down for some time, they landed and ravaged the flat country. Ethelwulph sent Wulfherd his general against them, who beat them back to their ships. The same year Æthelhelm, governor of Dorsetshire, routed another band which had disembarked at Portsmouth; and obtained the victory after a very furious engagement, but with the loss of his life.[6]

During the reign of Ethelred, he paid several subsidies to the invading Danes to induce them to depart. The money was levied upon the people in a tax called *Danegeldt*, and was the first money tax raised in Britain since the departure of the Romans, containing a space of more than 500 years.[7]

After the conversion of the Saxons to Christianity their ferocity began to abate, they became more peaceable, and a superstitious devotion succeeded that warlike disposition which so strongly marked their character. So greatly was the national character degenerated that a small party of Danes would attack and rout a numerous army of the English. To this change may be owing all the calamities and disgraces which afterwards befel them; "for when an Englishman met a Dane in a narrow path where he could not avoid him, he was obliged to stand still with his head uncovered and in a bending posture as soon as the Dane appeared, and to remain in that

---

their own families and property should, in the meantime be exposed by their absence to the fury of these barbarous ravagers. Every season of the year was dangerous; and the absence of the enemy was no reason why any man should esteem himself a moment in safety."— Vol. I. pp. 62, 63.

5 Of thirty-three sail. Sax. Ann.

6 HUME, vol. I. p. 62.

7 Hay's Hist. of Chichester.

posture till he was out of sight."[8] Indeed, we could hardly credit the abject submission of the English if the insolence of the one and the tameness of the other were not confirmed by other historians.[9]

In the year 897, Alfred fitted out nine ships against a squadron of Danish pirates that infested the coasts of Dorsetshire and Hampshire. On this occasion there ensued a sharp conflict between the two fleets, in which the Danes met with a total defeat, and the King ordered such of the crews who were made prisoners to be hanged along the sea coasts, as a terror to the rest of their marauding countrymen.[10]

A. D. 959. Edgar on his accession to the throne, desirous of securing his kingdom from all invasions of the Danes, determined to fit out a fleet, stronger than those of any of his predecessors; he accordingly augmented his navy to a number of ships that almost surpass the bounds of credibility. Some writers say it amounted to 4,800, but all agree that it consisted of at least 3,600 sail.[11] This fleet he divided into three squadrons or lesser fleets, consisting each of

---

8 Pontopopidon Gesta Danor. Tom. II. f. 139.

9 Sæpenumero decem aut duodecim Dani alternis vicibus uxorem, vel filiam, vel cognatam Thyani vitiant, ipso Thyano spectante, nec prohibere audente. Hick.—-THESAUR, T. I. p. 103.

10 Mortimer's Hist. Eng. Vol. I. p, 71.

11 Though the modern reader may be struck with astonishment at the greatness of this number, yet upon reflection we shall find it by no means incompatible with truth or probability, if we suppose (as we may reasonably do) that in this account is comprehended the whole of his naval force; and that every little cock-boat and pinnace is thrown in to add to the magnificence of the relation. To defray the expenses of this armament, he laid a tax on his subjects, and exacted a proper consideration from each of the petty princes who enjoyed the benefit of this valuable protection.— CAMPBELL's Lives of Eng. Adm. Vol.I.

1200 sail; and were stationed in such a manner, that they were continually cruizing round the island, by which prudent regulation he at once rendered his men complete sailors, and effectually covered his kingdom from any insults whatever.

During the reign of Ethelred II, the coasts of England were much pillaged by the Danes. The inactive Ethelred, instead of fitting out a fleet, or raising an army to oppose the progress of these invaders, had recourse to the dastardly expedient of giving them a sum of money[12] to depart. This he did by the advice of Siric, Archbishop of Canterbury, who, instead of rouzing Ethelred to a sense of honour, suffered him to indulge himself in that indolence which proved the opprobrium of his own name, and the destruction of his kingdom. For although the Danes, glad of the money which enabled them to continue their invasions with greater success, seemed for a time satisfied, yet this cowardly expedient was so far from answering the intended purpose, that it only served as a bait or allurement for others, who thought they had equal right to take advantage of the weakness of the English.[13]

A.D. 1001 the Danes returned to England, and committed the most horrid ravages. No place was free from their excesses; they burnt whole towns to the ground, and drove such of the inhabitants as they put not to the sword into the open fields, where these merciless invaders suffered them to perish for want of subsistence. They penetrated into the very interior of Hampshire, where they were met by Ethelward, at the head of the county militia; but the Danes, by the superiority of their numbers, gained the day, and the English were routed with the loss of many persons of distinction, among whom was Ethelward himself. They then passed over into the

---

12 £10,000.

13 Mortim. Hist. Eng. Vol. I. p. 91.

Isle of Wight, destroyed the town of Weltham and, availing themselves of some magazines they found there, again extended their irruptions over the most part of Hampshire and Devonshire. In short, by their merciless and successful ravages they seemed to threaten an extinction of the English name and nation; for not only all the southern parts were overrun by the foreign Danes, but the northern countries were peopled by the same nation, so that the unhappy English knew not which they had most reason to fear, the avowed enmity of the one, or the secret treachery of the other. In this extremity, Ethelred gave himself up to fear and despondence, and instead of endeavouring to oppose the enemy, summoned a council, A. D. 1002, and by their advice submitted once more to pay them a considerable sum of money on condition they desisted from their hostilities. The sum to be paid the Danes was fixed at £24,000, which was immediately raised by a tax on the people, distinguished by the name of *Dane gelt*;[14] a tax which afterwards became exceedingly burdensome to the nation, even for a long time after the Danes had quitted England.

This year, all the Danes in England were cruelly massacred. They

---

14 That is Danes Money; it was raised by a tax of twelve pence laid on every hide of land. A hide of land is by some authors calculated to be as much as can be ploughed by one plough in a year. Bede fixes it at as much as can maintain one family; some are so particular as to say, that it contained one hundred acres and others again assert that the number of acres was uncertain. This tax was afterwards named *Hildagium*, and then used as a general name for all taxes laid upon land. It was released by Edward the Confessor but levied again by William I and II, after which it was laid aside by Henry I and entirely abolished by Stephen. It is suggested that this ancient tax might probably be a precedent for our land tax of three or four shillings in the pound when first granted.

had indeed, behaved with great insolence, and treated the English with the utmost contempt, but nothing can purely justify the indiscriminate murder of any people. Ethelred, at the instigation of some infamous persons round him, conceived the horrid design and dispatched letters to every part of the kingdom; and the 13th day (or rather night) of November was fixed on for the completion of this detestable act. The bloody mandate was obeyed with the utmost punctuality; but as if heaven was resolved to manifest its displeasure, for the detestable piece of policy of which Ethelred and his subjects had been guilty, no sooner was the deed perpetrated, than the Danes appeared again upon our coasts, threatening the total destruction of the island; and after a series of defeats, he was conquered in 1014 by Swein, King of Denmark, who, seizing on the throne of England, was proclaimed king.[15]

From this period to 1066, Portsmouth suffered considerably from the predatory visits of the Danes; unmerciful butchery and wasting conflagration characterizing their exploits.

William the I, A.D. 1066, having meditated an invasion of this kingdom, Harold fitted out a fleet of 700 sail, which cruised about this harbour and the Isle of Wight; but the Norman fleet consisting of 300 vessels, large and small, and carrying an army of 60,000 men escaped them, and landed safe at Pevensey in Sussex.

Canute IV, A.D. 1086, having asserted a right to the crown of England, William raised a fleet to oppose him; but a mutiny breaking out among the soldiers of Canute, he was compelled to abandon his design. William being then at this place with his fleet took the advantage of a fair wind and set sail for Normandy.

In the beginning of the year 1101 an invasion was set on foot by Robert, Duke of Normandy, who by lawful inheritance claimed the

---

15 Mortimer's Hist. Eng. vol. I. p. 98. Hay's Hist. Chichester, p. 162.

crown of England; and having collected the whole Norman force, put
to sea with a fine fleet and landed at Portsmouth about the middle of
August, where he was received without opposition.

About this period, or soon after, Portsmouth seems to have
attained a considerable degree of importance; as the *Saxon Chronicle*
informs us that Henry I spent his Easter at Winchester and from
thence removed to Portsmouth, where he passed his Whitsun week
prior to his departure into Normandy.[16]

The death of Henry left the succession to be disputed by his
daughter, Matilda, or Maud, and Stephen Blois, son of the Earl of
Blois. The empress, taking advantage of the disturbances that arose
in England on the death of Henry, came over with the Earl of
Glocester and no more than one hundred and forty, about the end of
September, 1139, and landed at Portsmouth without opposition.[17]

Great disturbances arising between Philip, King of France, and
Philip, Earl of Flanders, King Henry II who was their guarantee and
umpire, went in March, 1182, to make peace between them; but prior
to his departure, he made his will near the sea side at Portsmouth,
one copy of which he put into his own treasury, one in the church of
Canterbury and another in the Treasury at Winchester.[18]

On the death of Henry II, A.D. 1189, his son Richard being at that
time in France, having settled all his affairs in that kingdom, landed
at Portsmouth on August 13th and hastening to London, was
solemnly crowned by Baldwin, Archbishop of Canterbury.[19] This
monarch, resolving to visit his foreign dominions and oppose the
French arms, embarked at Portsmouth on the 12th of May, 1194, with

16 Sax. Chron. Sim. Dunelm. Brompt.

17 Mortimer's Hist. Eng. Vol. I. p. 232

18 Hovedon, p. 614. Gervas, p. 1459. Rapin's Hist. Eng. Vol.1.

19 Mortimer's Hist. of Eng. Vol, I, p. 295.

a strong body of forces in a fleet of 100 large ships, and after a quick passage, landed safely at Barfleur.[20]

King John, finding his presence necessary on the Continent, summoned all his earls, barons and military tenants to attend him beyond sea by Whitsuntide, 1201, at Portsmouth, well provided with arms and horses. The kings of England were seldom accustomed to put their nobles to the trouble and expense of such foreign expeditions unless they had a war with some foreign potentate; and as the only business was now to crush two or three vassals of the crown, who had raised a commotion on account of some oppressions they had suffered, they refused to lend their assistance on this occasion; and having met in consultation at Leicester, they came to a resolution to send John word that they would not accompany him, unless he restored them their rights, which had been violated by a revival of the Forest Laws.

John, alarmed at this spirited resolution of his barons, commanded them to deliver up their castles. William de Albiney, the first nobleman of whom he exacted this demand, compounded for his Castle of Belvoir; and the rest upon paying a scutage of two marks for every knight's fee, were excused from the expedition. John, having despatched the Earl of Pembroke and the constable of Chester with 200 men at arms to suppress the revolters abroad, and appointed Hubert de Burgh guardian of the Welch marches during his absence, embarked with his queen Isabella at Portsmouth, in Whitsun week, and, after a tedious and dangerous passage, landed safely in Normandy.[21]

This monarch in the year 1213, having received authentic accounts of the resolution of Philip, King of France, to invade this kingdom,

---

20 Ibid, p. 311.

21 Mortimer's Hist. of Eng. Vol. I. p. 322.

resolved to take every necessary precaution to prevent his design. For this purpose he ordered a list to be taken of all the ships that were able to carry six horses, which were then in every port of England; and the masters thereof to bring them well manned, armed, and victualled, by a day appointed to Portsmouth, there to enter into his pay and service. He likewise sent to the sheriffs of every county in the kingdom to summon all the earls, barons, knights, esquires, vassals, whether holding of the crown, or of any other superior; and all who bore, or ought to bear arms, to come well provided with horses and accoutrements by the twenty-first of April, for the defence of his person and realm, under pain of being branded for cowards and deprived of the privileges of free men.

His orders were so urgent, and his threats had so sudden an effect, that in a little time he assembled more ships and forces than he could maintain, and was therefore compelled to dismiss part of his fleet. It was in the power of such a body of brave troops well affected to his cause to have defended their prince and country against the attempts of any potentate on earth, but unfortunately John knew better how to make himself feared than beloved; and at the head of this army he advanced to Dover, to receive Pandulph, the legate, who had passed sentence on him in France, and who was then coming to dethrone him in England.[22]

During the troubles between this monarch and the barons, the former, conceiving himself unsafe while in their custody, privately withdrew to this place and retired, attended only by seven attendants, to the Isle of Wight, where he had no sooner arrived than he publicly renounced all the obligations he had entered into with his subjects. In this situation of affairs, the barons desirous of putting an end to the calamities the country suffered, negotiated with the king,

---

22 Mortimer's Hist. of Eng. Vol I. p.335.

and at length a conference was appointed to be held between them. Oxford was the place pitched upon for this meeting, but John declined appearing on pretence of his person being unsafe among so many of his enemies; but the truth was that John had just received advice of the pope having issued a bull of excommunication against all who should dare to resist the king; and likewise that the foreign troops, whom he had sent to invite to his assistance, were ready to pass over to England.

He accordingly went on board a ship at Portsmouth and set sail for Dover, in order to meet this reinforcement, which arrived soon after in vast numbers from Brabant, Flanders and other parts of the continent. Thus strengthened, John put his subjects at open defiance and without loss of time set out at the head of his army and made himself master of Rochester, though not till after a very obstinate resistance, which so exasperated him that it was with considerable difficulty his generals persuaded him from putting the whole garrison to the sword in cold blood. However, William de Albiney, whom the barons had appointed governor of the castle, William of Lancaster, William de Emesford, and some others were sent close prisoners to Corfe Castle.[23]

---

23 Mortimer's Hist, of Eng. Vol. I. p. 359.

An accident happened during the siege, which confirms the upright intentions of the barons in general, in their opposition to the king, and reflects great honour on the character of Albiney himself. John and one of his principal officers reconnoitring the place, the person of the former was known by an excellent marksman, an engineer within the castle, who said to William de Albiney, "Sir, I have a dart here ready in my hand, shall I let fly at the king; I am sure of my mark?" — *"Heaven forbid!* (exclaimed de Albiney) *wretch that thou art! dost thou think that I would spill the blood of the Lord's anointed?"*

About the year 1224 the following (besides London) were esteemed the principal ports of England, as appears from the king's orders to the magistrates, in consequence of the expiration of a truce with France, to lay an embargo on all vessels lying in or arriving at the ports, and to keep them in readiness for the king's service:

Portesmue now Portsmouth	*Gipewic* now Ipswich
Sorham ... Soreham	*Lenne*... Lynne
Suhanton... Southampton	*Erewell*... Orwell
Safford... Seaford	*Eremuth*... Unknown
La Pole... Poole	*Dour*... Dover
Exon... Exeter	*Rumenel*... Rumley
Bristol... Bristol	*Rya*... Rye
Dertmue... Dartmouth	*Kingeston*... Unknown
Norwic... Norwich	*Eya*... Eye
Gerneniue... Yarmouth	*Hasting*... Hastings
Oreford... Orford	*Pageham*... Pagham
Dunewic... Dunwich	*Pevenses*... Pevensey[24]

A war with France breaking out in the year 1229, Henry III summoned all his earls, barons, and knights to meet him after Michaelmas at Portsmouth, where he assembled one of the finest armies that had ever been raised in England: nevertheless this extraordinary armament proved in vain, for when the troops came to be embarked, there were not ships enough to transport them. This

---

24 Anderson's Annals of Commerce, 4to Vol I. p. 385

disappointment threw the king into such a passion with Hubert de Burgh, who had engaged to get all things in readiness, that he called him an "Old Traytor," and would have killed him on the spot, had he not been prevented. It does not appear whether Hubert acted out of design or negligence, yet the embarkation was forced to be retarded the whole winter.

As soon, however, as the spring was come, for which Henry had waited with the utmost impatience, he embarked on 30th April (1230), with his army at this port, and landed at St. Maloes, May 3d, where he was received by the Earl of Bretagne[25].

But towards the end of the year 1231, the English army being reduced to a very inconsiderable number by intemperance, sickness, and various other causes, Henry determined to return home and accordingly made an engagement with the Earl of Bretagne by which he engaged to furnish that nobleman with cccc. knights and c. horse[26], as long as the war with France should continue, and to pay him 6000 marks immediately on his arrival in England. These articles being ratified, Henry embarked without delay, and landed at Portsmouth on the 26th of October.[27]

A..D. 1242. The mariners of the cinque ports making a very bad use of the commission given them by the king to annoy the subjects of France, wherein he warned them against injuring his own subjects, became pirates, and plundered all they met, not sparing even their own countrymen and relations. Nor were such atrocities confined only to the sailors of those Ports; there was a general combination of the inhabitants of the City of Winchester and the adjacent parts of

---

25 Rapin's Hist. of England, Vol. I.

26 [400 Knights and 100 horse]

27 Rapin's Hist. of England Vol. I. Mortimer's Hist. of England Vol. I. p. 409.

Hampshire, to plunder all whom they could overpower, whether Englishmen or foreigners, so that the king's own wine passing along in his carts could not evade their depredations. In consequence of a complaint made by two merchants of Brabrant, accompanied with threats of reprisal upon English merchants in that country, an inquisition was set on foot in the year 1249; but it was not without having recourse to very rigorous measures that a jury could be found to condemn the guilty, of whom about thirty were hanged[28].

This year likewise (1242) Henry again summoned all his military tenants to attend him with horses and arms at Portsmouth on the 27th of April, in order to embark for Guienne; and on the 15th of May embarked at this port with his Queen, Prince Richard, his brother, vii earls, ccc knights, and xxx hogsheads of silver[29]; and after an expeditious passage, landed at Santoigne, at the mouth of the river Gironde.

But in a short time, Henry, reduced to the extremity of want and deprived of all hopes of further remittances, began to prepare for his departure, and sent orders to all the nobility in England to assemble at Portsmouth to receive with joy their triumphant hero. They obeyed; but he made them wait so long that they were extremely disgusted by reason of the expense they were at during their stay.

At length, Henry embarked for England and, as the Roman Emperor after collecting cockle shells on the sea-shore, demanded and obtained the honour of a triumph. So, Henry entered London with as much pomp, parade, and magnificence,"as if he had returned from a conquest"[30].

A. D. 1253. This year, King Henry, having made preparations for a

---

28 Mat. Paris, pp. 589, 760

29 [7 earls, 300 knights and 30 hogsheads of silver.]

30 Mortimer's Hist. Eng. Vol. I. p. 423.

voyage to Gascony, commanded all his military tenants to attend him at this place, where no less than a thousand transports lay at Spithead ready to take on board the troops; and having appointed the Queen and the Earl of Cornwall co-regents of the kingdom in his absence, he set sail in the beginning of August with a very fine army[31].

A. D. 1273. The amount of a new duty called the *gauge*, at some of the chief ports of the kingdom, for the importation of wine, as made up from the Wednesday after Martinmas 1272 to Michaelmas 1273, gives us a pretty good idea of the quantity of foreign wine used in England at that period[32].

			Tuns
In *London*	£15 16 7	which at one penny per tun make	3,799
Southampton & Portsmouth	} £13 2 3	....	3,147
Sandwich	£7 18 4	....	1,900
	£36 17 2	The amount of gauge duty for	8,846

In the year 1295, a fleet of 350 or 360 ships was sent out to Guienne under the command of the Earls of Lancaster, Richmond and Lincoln. Three other squadrons, were likewise equipped to guard the coasts: the *Yarmouth*, or eastern, under John de Battletort; the *Portsmouth*, or southern, under William de Laybon, and the *Irish*, or western, whose commander is not named. The account of the force employed on this occasion becomes the more interesting from the

31 Mortim. Hist. Eng. Vol. I..p. 435.
32 Madox's Hist. Excheq. c. 18. sec 2.

circumstance not only of its affording the first specific information of the force and number of an English fleet, but because it contains very material internal evidence of the nature of the vessels employed, as well as their peculiar services; it stands also as an incontrovertible proof that the use of *gallies* was totally abandoned by the English[33].

This year (1295) *anno* 23 *Edward I.* The king ordered the sheriff of Southampton to provide with all speed cccc[34] quarters of wheat, to be collected in parts of his bailiwick nearest the sea, and to convey the same, being well winnowed, in good ships from *Portsmouth* to *Winchelsea.* Also to put on board the said ships at the same time, cc[35] tuns of cyder, the cost to be paid immediately from the king's wardrobe[36].

A.D. 1300. King Edward this year by the advice of his nobles entirely prohibited the currency of *pollards* and *crokards* and all other money not of his own coinage[37]. He also issued orders to the

---

33 Charnock's Marine Architecture, preface, pp. xxxiv xxxviii.

These fleets which were only formidable from their number, were fitted out by different monarchs, and were intended principally for invasion. On all such occasions, the vessels are not to be considered in any other light than as mere transports; they were not fitted out at the expense of the sovereign, but by different sea-ports, to whom certain privileges were granted, in consequence of their furnishing an established *quota* of vessels, whenever they were regularly demanded by the monarch.—CHARNOCK's Marine Architec. p. xxvi. *Vide* Appendix No 1

34 [400]

35 [200]

36 Warton's Hist. Eng. Poetry, Vol. I.

37 The king allowed *Pollards, Crokards* and *Rosaries* to go for an halfpenny each, before he totally prohibited them. But that reduction is not mentioned by *Trivet*, nor Matthew of *Westminster*; nor does any such reduction appear in the public records till the second year of Edward II. —

magistrates of all the ports in England to allow no money, either English or foreign, nor any bullion to be exported without his own special license; and from the orders issued on this occasion we obtain the following list of the ports of England, Wales, and that part of Scotland which was then under subjection to him[38].

Dover	Sidmouth	Harwich
Sandwich	Chichester	Ipswich
Romney	Teignmouth	Dunwich
Winchelsea	Frome	Orford
Rye	Fowy	Yarmouth
Hythe	Looe	Blackney
Faversham	Bodwyn	Lynne
Hastings	Haverford	Boston
Shoreham	Carmarthen	Wainfleet
Seaford	Caernarvon	Saltfleet
Portsmouth	Lanpadermaur	Grimsby
Southampton	Conway	Hull
Falmouth	Chester	Ravensere
Wareham	Bridgewater	Scarburgh
Bristol	Cardiff	Tinemouth
Dartmouth	Oystermouth	Newcastle upon Tine

MADOX's Excheq. c. 9. sec. 3.

38 Anderson's Annals of Commerce Vol. I. p. 464.

Weymouth	Rochester	Lymington
Poole	Gravesend	Bamburgh
Hamble	Northfleet	Berwick upon Tweed
Lyme	London	Dunbar[39]

King Edward, A.D. 1310, ordered the following Ports to send ships of war sufficiently equipped and manned to Dublin, in order to transport the Earl of Ulster and his forces to Scotland:

	Ships.		Ships.
Portsmouth to send	1	Colchester to send	1
Shoreham	1	Harwich	1
Lymington	1	Ipswich	2
Poole	1	Dunwich	1
Wareham	1	Orford	1
Weymouth	1	Yarmouth	6
Little Yarmouth	1	Dartmouth	1
Melcomb	1	Plymouth	1
Lyme	1	Snyterley	1
Exmouth and Exeter	1	Burnham and Holkam	1
Teignmouth	1	Boston	1
Grimsby	1	Newcastle-upon-Tyne	1

---

39 Ryley's Plac. Parl. p. 481

Lynne	4	Newby	1
Ravensere	1	Gloucester	1
Hull	2	Bristol	1
Scarburgh	1	Bridgewater	1
Hertlepool	1		

England was in the year 1315 afflicted by a most grievous famine, which raised the price of provisions far above the reach of the people of middling circumstances. The parliament, in compassion to the general distress, ordered that all kinds of food should be sold at moderate prices, which they took upon themselves to prescribe. The consequence was that all things, instead of being sold at or under the maximum price fixed by them, became dearer than before, or were entirely withheld from the markets. Poultry were rarely to be seen, butcher's meat was not to be found at all, the sheep were dying of a pestilence, and all kinds of grain were sold at most enormous prices. Early in the next year (1316), however, the parliament, perceiving their mistake, repealed their ill-judged act and left provisions to find their own price[40].

A.D. 1324. The King summoned the maritime towns on the south coast to assemble their largest vessels at Portsmouth, manned and

---

40 Walsingham, pp. 186, 187.

The prices affixed to the several kinds of provisions, by his act of parliament, were as follows: for the best ox not fed with corn, £2 8s of our present money; if fed with corn, £3 12s; a fat hog of 2 years old, 10s, a fat wether, unshorn, a crown; if shorn, three shillings and sixpence; a fat goose, sevenpence-halfpenny; a fat capon, sixpence; a fat hen, three-pence; two chickens three-pence; four pigeons, three-pence; 2 dozen of eggs, three-pence. — ROT. PARL. 7 Edw. II. N. 35, 36.

provided with landing bridges and *clays*[41], for carrying soldiers and horses, at his expense, over to his Duchy of Aquitaine; the following are the quotas ordered from each port:—

	Vessels		Vessels
Southampton	6	Poole	4
Sandwich	4	Seaford	2
Portsmouth	1	Weymouth	10
Winchelsea	6	Hamelhoke	1
Rye	2	Boldre	1
Faversham	1	Yarmouth	1

In the year 1336, a French fleet under the command of David King of Scotland scoured the English Channel, wasted the Isle of Wight, and threatened a descent on these parts. King Edward III, alarmed at these hostile measures, sent orders to all the maritime cities and towns in the kingdom, to oblige the owners to fit out every vessel in their ports in a sufficient manner, with arms, men, and stores, and appointed the harbour of Portsmouth to be the place of rendezvous for all vessels belonging to:

---

41 "Clayas," a word not well understood, meant perhaps for hurdles (*clayes* in French) for making temporary stalls for the horses; perhaps cleats (cross-bars) nailed upon the bridges to prevent the horses from slipping. In Rymer's *Fœdera*, Vol V. p. 6, I find the King orders the Sheriff to provide timber and brush ("buscam") for constructing *clays*, bridges, boards, racks, &c. for transporting horses; and in page 814, he orders 2,500 clays, ("claias") alone.

Portsmouth	Stonore	Teignmouth
Bristol	Sidmouth	Reculver
Christchurch	Sandwich	Exeter
Melcomb	Winchelsea	London
Southampton	Exmouth	Dover
Yarmouth	Bridgwater	Tallesbury
St. Helens	Chichester	Rye
Liverpool	Rumney	Seton
Lymington	Lyme	Plymouth
Pevensey	Seaford	Faversham
Weymouth	Dartmouth	Hastings
Chester	Porchester	Folkstone
Shoreham		

A.D. 1344. King Edward, desirous of being informed of the state of the navy, or shipping, of England, sent precepts to the magistrates of all the ports, ordering them to return a number of representatives, proportioned to their trade or commerce, well acquainted with maritime affairs, to a council of shipping, or naval parliament, to be held at London in the ensuing Lent; to which council it appears that Portsmouth sent one and Southampton two representatives.[42]

---

42 Rhymer's Fædera, vol v. p. 405.

At this period, *forty* men were deemed sufficient to man the best and largest vessels in England; Edward III's fleet before Calais in 1347 consisted of 788 English ships, carrying 14,956 mariners, being but 20 men to each ship; 15 ships and 459 mariners, being 30 men to each ship from Bayonne, 7

King Edward III, determining to prosecute the war with France with fresh vigour, issued orders to his military tenants in Ireland to furnish him with two hundred men at arms and five hundred light horse, and appointed the rendezvous of his fleet and forces at Portsmouth on Midlent Sunday, 1346; but by several accidents, they could not be assembled till the middle of May; and then he was prevented by contrary winds from executing his first design of landing in Guienne. While he continued wind-bound at Spithead, Geoffrey de Harcourt, who attended him, persuaded him to alter the plan of his operations and to make a descent upon Normandy, a plentiful country, which had been long exempted from the calamities of war.

Edward, who relished this advice, hesitated not to comply with it; and as soon as the wind proved fair, sailed from St. Helens, and after

---

ships and 184 men from Spain, which is 26 men to each ship; 1 from Ireland, carrying 25 men; 14 from Flanders, with 133 men, not 10 men to each ship; and 1 from Guelderland, with 24 mariners; 15 of these were called the King's own ships, manned with 419 mariners, being somewhat under 17 to each ship. The total number was 776 ships and 15,781 mariners, being on an average but 21 men to each ship.

In 1345, when Edward III was raising a fleet for the invasion of France, we have the following list of the proportionate ship to be furnished by the various ports of Hampshire.

	Ships	Men
Isle of Wight	13	220
Portsmouth	5	96
Hannilhoke (now Hamble-heek)	11	208
Southampton	21	576
Lymington	9	159

a passage of only two days, landed at La Hogue.[43]

The commons in the year 1372, represented in parliament that ships were often taken up for the King long before they were wanted, and the merchants ruined by supporting their seamen in idleness; that by the merchants, the supporters of the navy, being so often deprived of their ships, the mariners were driven into other trades; and that the masters of the king's vessels pressed the masters of

---

43 He set sail the 4th of June, 1346; but was driven back again by a storm. His army consisted of 4,000 men at arms, 10,000 archers, 12,000 Welsh infantry, and 6,000 Irish, besides a great number of the chief nobility, whose names may be seen in Froissart. Knyghton says he had 1,600 ships, great and small. On this occasion his cities and towns supplied him with certain numbers of well armed men, who were to enter into the King's pay at their embarkation at Portsmouth. The *quota* furnished by each city was as follows.

London: 100 men at arms, who, in those times, were on horseback, and in armour, attended each by three or four men armed, on foot, as that might amount to five hundred in all; and five hundred armed soldiers.

Footsoldiers each:

Norwich	120
Bristol	60
Coventry	40

30 footsoldiers each: Oxford, Shrewsbury, Hereford, St. Edmundsbury, Winchester, Salisbury, Exeter

Northampton 25

20 each: Cambridge, Gloucester, Worcester , Reading, Chichester, Bodmyn

15 each: St. Albans, Wells, Launceston,

12 each: Leicester, Shaftesbury,

10 each: Baldock, Huntingdon, Ludlow, Abingdon, Bedford, Rochester, Maidstone, Barnstaple, Honiton.

other vessels, as good men as themselves, whereby the men were also obliged to seek other means of living, and the ships were rendered useless, and that by these means the navy was reduced. Notwithstanding this remonstrance, the king issued orders for all vessels in England and Wales to enter into his service and to assemble on or before the first day of May in the harbour of Portsmouth, opposite the Isle of Wight[44].

Upon the death of Edward III, Richard II was crowned, A.D. 1377, in which year the French landed at Portsmouth, which they plundered and burnt[45], but the inhabitants furiously attacked them and drove them back to their ships with great precipitation and slaughter. After this unexpected defeat, they landed in the Isle of Wight and sailing round to Plymouth, they destroyed that and several other towns and villages on the coast[46].

A.D. 1386, the Duke of Lancaster, having completed his preparations for an expedition to Spain, repaired to Portsmouth with his Princess in order to embark; but contrary winds detained him till the month of July, when he finally set sail with an army of 20,000 men at arms, and 8,000 archers[47]. He carried with him Constantia of

---

44 RYMER, Vol. VI page 708

45 Normani intraverunt cum magna potentia in Portesmuth, et miserint in flammam ignis totam villam.— HEN. DE KNYGHTON.

46 Froissart, speaking of the French fleet prepared for the invasion of England in the reign of Richard II says that the ships were painted with the arms of the commanders, and gilt, with banners, pennons, and standards of silk; and that the masts were painted from top to bottom glittering with gold; the ship of Lord Grey of Tremayll, was so sumptuously garnished that the painting and colours cost 2000 French franks, more than £212 of English currency at that time —-Vide Appendix No. II.

47 According to Froissart, he had 1,287 ships of all sorts; and according

Castile his wife, and his two daughters, Philippa and Catherina; King Richard II and his Queen accompanied them to Portsmouth and, wishing them success, presented them with two gold crowns; after which he set sail, and arrived on August the 9th at Corunna, where he landed his troops[48].

In the year 1416, a number of French ships came and blocked up the English fleet at Portsmouth, which was destined for the invasion of France, under the command of Henry V; they also made an attempt on the Isle of Wight, but were repulsed[49]. This year likewise King Henry V, having mustered his army at Southampton, sailed from this port on July the 27th and landed at Beville in Normandy on August the 1st[50].

A treaty of marriage having been concluded on between Henry VI and Margaret of Anjou, daughter of Regnier Duke of Anjou and Lorraine, this princess was conducted to England, attended by the Marchioness of Suffolk and a large train of nobility, and landed at Portsmouth, from whence she went to the priory at Southwick and was there married on the eighteenth of April, A.D. 1445[51].

In the year 1475, this town is remarkable for a review which took place on South-sea common of no less than 30,000 men under the command of King Edward IV, who directed letters to all the sheriffs and magistrates in England to assemble his whole army at Portsmouth by the 26th of May[52].

From an indenture of war made in the year 1492, we find that

---

to others, no less than 60,000 fighting men. — WALS. TYRREL.

48 Rapin's Hist. Eng. Vol.I. p. 427.

49 Goodwin, pp. 106, 107.

50 Ibid. p. 155

51 Mortimer's Hist. Eng. Vol. II. p. 67.

52 Ibid. p. 114

George, Earl of Kent, engaged to serve King Henry VII abroad in such places as he shall direct for one whole year, with six men of arms, each man having with him his *custrill* and page, sixteen demi-launces, sixteen archers on horseback, and sixty archers on foot, all able men fit for service, properly horsed, armed and arrayed; the whole to be mustered at Guildford on the 4th of June, and on their arrival at Portsmouth, the rendezvous of the army to receive the conduct money, which was an allowance for marching to be calculated at the rate of vi d for every xx[53] miles each soldier should march, to be reckoned from his residence to Portsmouth, each Soldier to swear to the number of miles marched by him. And that from the first day that the said earl should arrive at Portsmouth, and during the time he should serve the king in his wars, he should receive for every man at arms, garnished with his custrill and page, i s vi d[54] by the day; for every demilaunce, ix d[55] and for every archer vi d[56]. The earl to receive a month's pay in advance, immediately on his arrival at Portsmouth, to be paid without any deduction before the transports left the harbour[57].

It appears, by a statute enacted in the year 1541, and in which a number of decayed cities and towns is exhibited, that there had been in times past many beautiful houses within the walls and liberties of Portsmouth, "which houses are now fallen down, decayed, and at this time remain unre-edified as desolate and vacant grounds, many of them nigh adjoining the high street, replenished with much uncleanness and filth, with pits, cellars and vaults lying open, and

---

53[Sixpence for every 20 miles.]

54 [One shilling and sixpence.]

55 [Nine pence.]

56 [Sixpence.]

57 Gross's.Military Antiquities, Vol. I. p. 285.

uncovered; to the great peril of the king's subjects; and other houses are in danger of falling, &c[58]."

Leland the antiquary, having made a perambulation through England, has left the following description of this town, when he visited it in the reign of Henry VIII:—

"The land heere (says he) on the east side of portesmuth hauen rennith farther by a great way strait into the se, by south-est from the hauen mouth, than it doeth at the weste poynte. There is at this poynte of the hauen, Portesmuth towne, and a great round toure, almost double in quantite and strenkith to that, that is on the west side of the hauen right agayn it; and here is a mighty chaine of yron, to draw from tourre to tourre. About a quarter of a mile above this tourre is a great dok for shippes, and yn this dok lyeth part of the rybbes of the *Henrie Grace of Dieu*, one of the biggest shippes that hath been made in hominum memoria. Ther be above this dok crekes in this part of the hauen.

"The towne of Portesmuth is mured from the est tour a forough lengthe, with a mudde waulle armid with tymbre, wheron be great peaces both of yron and brassen ordinauns; and this peace of waulle having a diche without it, runnith so far flat, south south-est, and is the place moste apte to defende the toun ther open on the hauen. Ther rennith a diche almost flat est for a space, and wythin it is a waulle of mudde like to the other, and so theus goith rounde aboute the toun to the circuite of a mile. Ther is a gate of tymbre at the north

---

58 Anderson's Ann. Com. Vol. II. p. 88.

The author in his observations on this Act of Parliament, very justly supposes, that the nuisances complained of, were more the result of carelessness, than owing to any real decay in the cities and towns mentioned in the statute; since it is well known that many of them were at this very time increasing in opulence and manufactures.

est ende of the toun, and by it is cast up an hille of erthe diched, wherein be gunnes to defend entre into the toun by land. Ther is much vacant ground wythin the toun waulle. Ther is one fair streate in the toune from west to north est.

"I learnid in the toun, that the tourres in the haun mouth were begon in King Edwarde IV tyme, and set forwarde in building by Richard the III. King Henry the VIII ended them at the procuration of Fox Bishop of Winchester. King Henrie the VIII at his first warres into Fraunce, erected in the southe part of the toune vii great brewing houses, with the implements to serve his shippes at such tyme as they should go to the se in tyme of warre. One Carpenter, a riche man, made of late tyme, in the mydle of the Highe Streate of the toun, a toun-house. *The toun is bare, and little occupied in tyme of peace[59]*."

In the thirty sixth year of this monarch's reign[60], the French landed with 2,000 men, under the command of D'Annebaut, in the Isle of Wight. It was their intention to take possession and fortify it for the king of France; but they were unsuccessful and driven back to their ships with the loss of their Admiral and a great part of his forces[61].

---

59 Lel. Itin. Vol. III. pp. 81, 82.

60 [1545]

61 It was the *first* intention of D'Annebaut to *destroy* the town of Portsmouth. The English fleet, under Viscount Lisle in the Great Marry, anchored off Spithead to receive them, and a distant cannonade continued for two days between the adverse fleets; but the French at length began to retreat, and after plundering part of the Isle of Wight, retired to their own coasts. During the engagement, the *Mary Rose*, one of the largest of the English ships, and commanded by *Sir George Carew*, overpowered by the weight of her own ordnance, and heeling greatly, the water rushed in at her

Henry VIII was the first monarch under whom the navy obtained a systematic establishment. In the preceding reigns the naval force *"was either hired from the merchant, foreign or native, or supplied by the cinque and other ports of the Kingdom; but the navy was under no sort of regulation: the bargain was made with the first, or the demand made from the last, according to their different assessments.*[62]"

Henry VII, indeed, appears to have made Portsmouth a Royal Dock; but no regular system was entered into before the time of his successor to render the navy a national concern. Even in the time of Edward VI, Portsmouth was almost the *only* naval station and the only dock yard that could be considered as a national one. All the ships that Britain could then boast, and which including galleys, pinnaces, and row-barges, were 43, lay at this port; with the exception of two at Deptford Strand, and one, the *Henry Grace de Dieu* at Woolwich. The whole number of men belonging to these vessels, including soldiers, marines and gunners, was 7780[63].

Among the number of royal visitors who have honoured Portsmouth with their presence may be reckoned King Edward VI, as appears from his letter to his friend Barnaby Fitz Patrick, written during his progress in 1552.

"From thes (writes the youthful Sovereign) we wente to Portismouth toune, and there viewed not only the toune itself, and the hauen, but also divers bulwarkes: in viewing of which, we find the bulwarkes chargeable, massie, and ramparted, but il facioned, il flanked, and set in unmete places; the toune weake in comparison of that it ought to be; the hauen notable greate, and standing by nature

---

port-holes, and sunk her.

62 Pennant's Journey to the Isle of Wight, Vol. II. p. 137.

63 Vide Appendix, No. III.

easie to be fortified. And for the more strength therof, we have devised two strong castellis on either side of the hauen, at the mouth therof; for at the mouth of the hauen is not past ten score ouer, but in the middle almoste a mile ouer, and in length, for a mile and a hauf, liable to bear the greatest ship in Christendome."

In the year 1623 Charles, Prince of Wales, (afterwards Charles I) and the Duke of Buckingham, returned from their dangerous travels in France and Spain, and after escaping a violent storm, landed at Portsmouth on the fifth of October, where he was received with the greatest joy imaginable.

In the year 1628 Portsmouth was appointed as the rendezvous of the armament destined to relieve the protestants in Rochelle, then besieged by Cardinal Richelieu; and the fleet being ready to sail, the Duke of Buckingham repaired to Portsmouth to take command of it. One Felton, a man of good family, but of a gloomy enthusiastic disposition, had served as a lieutenant under the duke in his late expedition to Rhé. His captain being killed in the retreat, Felton applied to Buckingham for the company; but being refused, he threw up his commission and retired discontented from the army. The remonstrance of the Commons against Buckingham encouraged at once his resentment and enthusiastic fury; he was now convinced it would be a meritorious action in the sight of heaven to murder him, whom the Parliament had accused as the author of all the misfortunes of his country.

Filled with these ideas, he repaired to Portsmouth, fully determined to execute his murderous design.

Early in the morning of the 23d of August, Buckingham received intelligence that a small convoy of provisions had got safe into Rochelle; this news he communicated to the Duke of Saubise and the French gentlemen in his train, who insisted with great vehemence that the whole was false, and intended only to retard the sailing of the fleet. During these asseverations, the duke drew towards the door, and turning himself in the passage to speak to Sir Thomas Fryer, a Colonel in the army, he was stabbed by an unknown hand over Sir Thomas's shoulder. The knife with which the wound was inflicted reached his heart, and without uttering any other words than "the villain has killed me", he drew out the knife and immediately expired in a deluge of his own blood.

As no person had seen the hand that had given the blow, it was supposed that the murder had been committed by one of the French Gentlemen whose angry tone of voice had been heard, while their words were not understood by the people. Some were for putting them to death immediately, but were prevented by the more considerate part, who thought it highly reasonable they should undergo a lawful trial.

In the midst of this confusion a hat was found near the door, in the inside of which was sewed a paper containing three or four lines of the remonstrance of the Commons, which declared Buckingham an enemy to the kingdom. All were now convinced that this hat belonged to the assassin, but there was a sufficient reason to think he had escaped far enough during the tumult not to be found without a hat. They were, however, mistaken; Felton never attempted to escape from justice, and he was soon perceived walking leisurely before the door, without his hat. He was immediately seized, confessed the murder, and seemed to triumph in the action. The enraged soldiers drew their swords and were for immediately sacrificing him on the spot. Their fury had no effect upon Felton, he readily exposed his breast to their anger: its effects were, however, prevented, and the assassin secured.

Some being desirous of finding whether Felton had any

accomplices, hinted that Buckingham, though dangerously wounded, was not dead; but that there were great hopes of his recovery. Felton smiled at this and replied in words very expressive of his enthusiasm, *"I know that he is dead, for I had the force of forty men when I struck the blow."* When questioned with regard to the persons by whose authority he had perpetrated the horrid deed, he told them that enquiries were useless, that no person on earth had sufficient influence to have disposed him to undertake such an action; that no man living was privy to his purpose; that the resolution proceeded wholly from the impulse of his own conscience; and that if his hat was found, his motives would sufficiently appear; for, persuaded he should perish in the attempt, he had taken care to explain them in order that no innocent person might suffer on his account.

Reflection and confinement, however, had great effect on the enthusiastic spirit of Felton; he seemed to recover from his delusion, expressed remorse for what he had done, and suffered death with composure and resignation[64].

King Charles I, having determined in the year 1634 to fit out a formidable fleet, commanded the City of London to send to Portsmouth, at their own cost, the following quota of ships, for 26 weeks; and the like commands were sent to many other sea-port towns in the kingdom:—

One ship of 900 tons, and 350 men;
One ship of 800 tons, and 260 men;

---

64 Felton was hung in chains on South-sea Common; not many years since his gibbet was still visible; there are now however no remains left of it. The murder of the Duke was committed, at NO. 10 in the High-street, at present the residence of the Rev. G. Cuthbert: the house, which then comprehended the houses on each side, was at that time a large Inn, known by the name of the *"Spotted Dog"*.

Four ships each of 500 tons, and 200 men;

And one ship of 300 tons, and 150 men.

This, in all probability, was the first year of that monarch's project of ship-money, which afterwards became one of the principal causes of his ruin[65].

When the civil wars broke out between Charles I and his Parliament, this town, being considered as a place of great importance, was seized on by the latter; but it was one of the first that declared for Charles II upon his restoration to the crown; and he was accordingly on the 12th of May, 1660 "*p'laymed Kinge of England, Scotlande, Fraunce, and Irelande, &c. at Portesmuth wt verie great solemnity.*"

In the year 1662, Catherine, the consort of King Charles II landed here from Lisbon, where she waited five days before the King's arrival, when they were married by Dr. Sheldon, in the Governor's chapel. As it may gratify the curious, we insert the following extract of a letter, from Charles II to Lord Clarendon, on his marrying the Queen at Portsmouth:—

"Portsmouth, 21st May, 8 in the Morning.

" I arrived here yesterday about two in the afternoon, and as soon as I had shifted myself, I went to my wife's chamber... her face is not so exact as to be called a beauty, though her eyes are excellent good, and not anything in her face that in the least can *shocque* one. On the contrary, she has as much agreeableness in her looks altogether, as ever I saw; and if I have any skill in physiognomy, which I think I have, she must be as good a woman as ever was born. Her conversation, as much as I can perceive, is very good; for she has wit enough, and a most agreeable voice. You would much wonder to see

---

65 And. Ann. Com. Vol. II. p. 378.

how well we are acquainted already. In a word, I think myself very happy; but, I am confident our two humours will agree very well together: I have not time to say any more. My Lord Lieutenant will give you an account of the rest."

It appears from the following list of ships at Portsmouth on June 19th, A.D. 1684, that this port was still more and more encreasing in national importance, and was at that time the only place of naval rendezvous in the kingdom:

1st Rate.

Royal Charles

Royal James

Charles

2d Rate.

French Ruby

Ossory

Vanguard

3d Rate.

Dunkirk	Plymouth
Dreadnought	Swiftsure
Edgar	Warspite
Expedition	York
Harwich	Eagle
Lyon	Northumberland
Monk	

4th Rate.

Advice	Kingsfisher
Bristol	Reverse
Jersey	

5th Rate

Rose

Guarland

Swan

6th Rate
Fann Fann

Fire-ships.

Ann & Christopher	Yacht
Castle	Merlin
Sampson	Hulks
Sarah	America
Young Spragg	Slothany

A.D. 1688. William of Orange (afterwards William III) being called over by the people of England to accept the Crown, on his passage hither with a fleet of fifty men of war, twenty-five frigates, as many fire-ships, and between three and four hundred victuallers and transports, having on board them 4,000 horse and 9,000 foot passed by this place and the Isle of Wight and arrived safe in November at Torbay.

This monarch having received intelligence of the landing of James II in Ireland in the following year, despatched Admiral Herbert from Spithead, where he was then stationed, with twelve ships of the line, one fire-ship and four tenders, to intercept a strong squadron under the command of Admiral Chateau Renaud, who was conveying to him arms and ammunition. The Admiral came up to them on the coast of Ireland, and having dispersed them, returned to Portsmouth. The king was so satisfied with Admiral Herbert's conduct on this occasion that he visited this place and not only dined on board the Elizabeth, the Admiral's ship, but declared to him his intention of creating him an Earl in consideration of his services[66].

Spithead in the year 1692 was appointed the rendezvous of the armament against France. Admiral Russel lay here with a large squadron, expecting the arrival of the Dutch fleet under Admiral Allemonde, who joined him about the middle of May. While they remained at St. Helen's, Admiral Russel received a letter from the Earl of Nottingham, as Secretary of State, written by direction of Queen Mary, in which he was informed, "That a scandalous and malicious report was spread, as if some of the officers of their Majesties' fleet were disaffected, or not hearty in their service, and that her Majesty had been thereupon induced to order the discharge of many of them, but her Majesty charged the Admiral to acquaint his officers that she was satisfied this report was raised by the enemies of the government, and that she reposed an entire confidence in their fidelity and had resolved to displace notsomuch as one of them."[67] Upon this, the flag-officers and captains drew up a very dutiful and loyal address, dated from on board the Britannia, at St.Helen's, May 15th, 1692, which was transmitted to court and presented to her Majesty by the Lords of the Admiralty, to which she returned this gracious answer : "I always had this opinion of the commanders, but I am glad this is come, to satisfy others."

William III, on the 16th of February, 1693, visited Portsmouth, took a view of the fleet then at Spithead, and dining on board with Vice-Admiral Rook, conferred on him the honour of knighthood. The following year, Admiral Russel, being appointed to the command of the fleet, sailed from Spithead on the third of May, with the combined squadrons, consisting of 52 English, and 41 Dutch sail of the line, besides frigates, fire-ships and other smaller vessels.

---

66 Mortim. Hist. Engl. Vol. III. p. 11.

67 Campbell's Lives of the Admirals, Vol. III. p, 63.

In the year 1703, on the 26th of November, about eleven o'clock at night, a most violent storm arose here, such as had never been known in the memory of man, attended with such flashes of lightning and peals of thunder as filled every mind with the utmost terror and consternation. The houses shook from their foundations, and many of them falling, overwhelmed the inhabitants in their ruin. The Newcastle, a fourth-rate ship, commanded by Capt. Carter, was lost at Spithead. The carpenter and thirty-nine men were preserved; the rest, consisting of *one hundred and ninety-three*, were unhappily drowned. The *Vesuvius* fire-ship was likewise lost at Spithead, but all her crew were saved. It is supposed that there perished in this storm, in different parts of the kingdom, no less than thirteen ships and upwards of 1500 seamen, among whom was Rear-Admiral Beaumont, who had been employed this year in reconnoitring the French squadron at Dunkirk.

On the 23d of December 1703, Charles III of Spain arrived at Spithead and on the following day the Duke of Somerset, master of the horse to the Queen, waited on him aboard with a letter of compliment from her Majesty, and acquainted him, she expected to see him at Windsor. The next day Charles landed at the point, and on December the 29th he arrived at Windsor about seven o'clock at night, where he was most graciously received by the Queen. His Catholic Majesty being very desirous however of prosecuting his voyage to Lisbon, returned to Portsmouth on the thirty-first of the same month, and the next day went on board the *Royal Catherine*, commanded by Admiral Rooke. The Dutch squadron arrived at Spithead on the 5th of January 1704, the combined fleet set sail for Portugal; but before they had reached *Cape Finisterre*, the admiral was driven back by the storm to Spithead, and compelled to remain there till the middle of February; and then being favoured with a fair wind, he set sail and arrived there on the twenty-fifth of the same month.

A. D. 1708. It being resolved on this year, to make a descent on, and alarm the coast of France; the fleet, with the transports having the troops on board, intended for the descent, sailed from Spithead on the 20th July under the command of Admiral Sir George Byng; and after hovering some days on the French coast, they anchored on the 11th of August in the bay of La Hogue, with an intention of landing; but upon reconnoitring the coast they found so strong a force collected to oppose the descent and so many forts and batteries in a condition to defend the shore that it was deemed impracticable, and accordingly the fleet on the 28th of August returned to Spithead[68].

In the year 1727 an armament was got ready at Portsmouth intended to be employed against Spain, under the command of Sir Charles Wager. The Earl of Portmore, Governor of Gibralter, notwithstanding his advanced age, having been a colonel near forty years, resolved to repair in person to his government and accordingly arriving at Portsmouth, embarked on board this fleet; which sailing in the month of March, arrived at Gibralter, the place of their destination, in the beginning of April.

A.D. 1740. This year a very powerful fleet consisting of twenty-one sail of the line and three fire ships was assembled at Portsmouth, destined for a secret expedition; and on the 24th of June, Sir John Norris, admiral of the red, hoisted his flag on board the Victory, a first rate ship of 110 guns, having under him Philip Cavindish Esq, admiral, and Sir Chaloner Ogle, rear-admiral of the blue. The destination of this fine fleet was variously conjectured, but whatever were the real motives, the project came to nothing. After the fleet had

---

68 Mortimer, Vol. III. p. 531.

been detained about a week at Spithead by contrary winds it sailed from thence on the 14th of July, with the convoy and merchant ships, for Portugal and the Streights. But, meeting with some hard gales, in which the *Lion* man of war of 60 guns ran foul of the *Victory* and carried away her bowsprit, the fleet returned to St. Helen's and on the 22d sailed again, but was detained for nearly a month at Torbay. At last on the 30th of September the fleet returned to Spithead; and thus ended a very expensive armament which had engrossed the whole attention of all Europe, without having effected any one purpose it had undertaken. In September also the same year another noble fleet was assembled here, under, the command of Sir Chaloner Ogle, consisting of twenty-one sail of the line, besides frigates and fire-ships, with about 12, 000 sailors on board, detachments of foot soldiers, and six regiments of marines, of which Lord Cathcart was appointed commander-in-chief. They were likewise furnished with hospital-ships, store-ships, and all kinds of warlike implements. This fleet, however, did not sail till the latter end of October, by which delay they were incapable of getting through the channel till the Spaniards had strengthened their settlements in the West Indies.

In the year 1747, Rear Admiral Hawke arrived on the 31st of October at Portsmouth, with the six French prizes he had captured on the coast of Brittany; and it was into this port that within the space of five months the flower of the French Navy was triumphantly conducted; in consideration of which services, and of his gallant behaviour on those occasions, Admiral Hawke was created a Knight of the Bath.

The town of Portsmouth in the year 1750 was thrown into the utmost consternation by the shock of an Earthquake: on the 18th of March, between five and six o'clock in the evening, the town was alarmed by a shock, attended by a hollow and rustling noise like that of wind, providentially however, no mischief happened except the throwing down several chimnies and damaging some houses.

A. D. 1756. On the third of July, the unfortunate Admiral Byng was brought into Spithead and put under an arrest, in order to be tried by a Court Martial, which took place on December the 28th. Upon summing up the evidence, the court were of opinion that his misconduct arose neither from cowardice nor disaffection and therefore earnestly recommend him to mercy. They also added the following remonstrance to the Lords of the Admiralty in his favour:-

"We the undersigned, the president and members of the court-martial, assembled for the trial of Admiral Byng, believe it unnecessary to inform your lordships, that in the whole course of this long trial, we have done our utmost endeavour to come at truths, and to do the strictest justice to our country and the prisoner, but we cannot help laying the distresses of our minds before your lordships on this occasion, in finding ourselves under the necessity of condemning a man to death, from the great severity of the 12th article of war, part of which he falls under, and which admits of no mitigation, even if the crime should be committed by an error of judgment only; and therefore for our own consciences sakes, as well as in justice to the prisoner, we pray your Lordships, in the most earnest manner, to recommend him to his Majesty's clemency."

Notwithstanding this remonstrance, and the petitions of Lord Torrington, nephew to the unhappy Admiral, and other persons of high distinction, they proved ineffectual, and he was, pursuant to his sentence, executed on the 14th of March, 1757, on board his Majesty's ship Monarque, in Portsmouth harbour; and in his last moments conducted himself with a dignity and fortitude that never inspired a breast infected with cowardice, or conscious of guilt.

A.D. 1757. An armament was fitted out on a secret expedition, consisting of eighteen ships of the line, besides frigates, fireships, bomb-ketches, and transports, under the command of Sir Edward Hawke. The embarkation of the troops was, however, obstructed for several weeks, from various circumstances, and particularly from the circumstance of a sufficient number of transports not having arrived.

At last, the transports arrived, the troops were put onboard with all expedition, and the fleet got under sail on the eighth of September.

On the 17th of November, 1759, the corpse of General Wolfe, who was killed before the walls of Quebec, was brought on shore from Spithead with the highest naval and military honours. Landing a little after nine, it was put into a hearse, and followed by some attendants in a mourning coach. At the Fountain Inn, a coach with the General's two *Aids-de-Camp* stood ready, and followed the hearse from thence through the town till they were on the outside of the Landport Gate, when the hearse and coach set forward towards London.

Early on Tuesday morning, the 22d of June, 1773, his present Majesty set out from Kew for Portsmouth, and being arrived at Portbridge between ten and eleven the same morning, was welcomed by a royal salute of twenty-one guns. His Majesty then proceeded to the first barrier, where Major-General Parker delivered the keys of the garrison to him, who returned them. On his entering the Landport Gate, he was saluted with a triple discharge of 232 pieces of cannon. He passed through the town to the Commissioner's house in the Dock-yard, where he was received by many of the nobility. The artificers of the yard being all assembled before the house, gave three cheers as he entered, and then immediately returned to their several employments; and after taking some refreshment, his Majesty, with his retinue, went to the Governor's house in the town and had a public levee[69], at which numbers of all ranks were present.

The Mayor and Corporation waited on him with an address, were graciously received, and kissed his hand; the honour of knighthood being conferred on the Mayor, John Carter, Esq. The levee ended, the King returned to the Dock-yard and from thence proceeded in a barge to Spithead, accompanied by the Board of Admiralty, the three Admirals with their Flags and all the Captains of the fleet in their respective barges. As he passed by the garrison he was saluted with 21 guns, and when the standard was seen by the fleet at Spithead, consisting of 20 ships of the line, 2 frigates, and 3 sloops, the whole saluted with 21 guns each.

The King went on board the *Barfleur*, of 90 guns, the standard was then hoisted at the main-top-mast head, and saluted with 21 guns by all the ships. After having viewed the ship, at half-past three o'clock, his Majesty sat down to dinner, after which, the Queen's health being drank, the whole fleet saluted with 21 guns; and upon his quitting the table, his health was drank with the like salute. His Majesty at six -o'clock went into his barge, the other barges attending as before, and passed every ship, each saluting him with 21 guns. He then went on board the *Augusta* yacht and sailed into the harbour, attended with the barges and saluted as upon his coming out.

On Wednesday, his Majesty viewed the Dock-yard, harbour and ships in ordinary, and afterwards went to Spithead to dine on board the *Barfleur*, and returned in the evening accompanied as before.

On Thursday, he viewed the Gun wharf, different parts of the Dock-yard, the brewery and magazines. After which, he had another public levee at the Governor's house, from whence he proceeded in the same state as on the preceeding days, to dine on board the *Barfleur*. Many were knighted this day. In the evening he returned to

---

69 [A levee is a reception]

the Dock, as on the former days.

On Friday, he viewed the new works and fortifications of Portsmouth and then sailed out of the harbour in the *Augusta* yacht, being saluted in his passage. On his arrival at Spithead, Lord Edgcomb, with his division, got under sail and followed his Majesty; the yacht proceeded as far as Sandown Bay, then it returned to St. Helen's and from thence to Spithead, leaving his Lordship to proceed to Plymouth, according to previous orders.

After this, the King stood towards the harbour and anchored near Southsea beach. While the yacht was at anchor, the land forces, from the ramparts, at 10 o'clock fired a *feu de joie* by a triple discharge of cannon and musquetry all round the line, after which, his Majesty landed at the Dock. Several promotions were made this day. The sea and shores were covered with an innumerable number of vessels and people each day.

On Saturday, a quarter before seven in the morning, his Majesty set out from thence on his return to Kew, where he arrived about two in the afternoon. He was saluted by a triple discharge of cannon, as at his entrance, many thousand person attending, with the loudest acclamations. He left £1500 to be distributed to the artificers of the different departments; £350 to the seamen of the *Barfleur's* yacht and of his barge; and £250 to the poor. He released the prisoners also confined for debt. He expressed the highest approbation of the good order and discipline of his fleet, of the excellent condition of the Dock-yard, &c., and of the regularity with which every thing was conducted; and showed the utmost satisfaction at the demonstrations of loyalty and affection with which he was received by all ranks of people.

In the month of August, 1782, a, fleet was hastily equipped at Portsmouth destined for an expedition to Gibralter. Previously to its sailing, it was found necessary that the *Royal George*, of 108 guns, commanded by the gallant Admiral Kempenfeldt and long held as the first ship in the British navy, should receive a sort of slight careening; in which process, a ship is laid in a certain degree on her side, while the defects under water are rectified. This business was undertaken early in the morning of the 29th of August. The carpenter finding it necessary to strip off more of her sheathing than was at first expected, their eagerness to come at the leak induced them to heel her rather more on her side than had been intended. The ship, as is usually the case on coming into port, was crowded with people from the shore, particularly women, who were not estimated at less than 300. Among these, were many of the wives and children of the seamen and petty officers who, knowing that the fleet was to sail on distant and perilous service, eagerly embraced the opportunity of coming to see their husbands and fathers. Between eight and nine hundred of the crew of the Royal George, including marines, were then on board.

In this situation, about ten in the morning, the Admiral, being writing in his cabin, and much the greater part of the people happening then to be between decks, a sudden and unexpected squall of wind threw the ship fatally on her side, and her gun ports being open, and the motion of the cannon probably increasing the violence of the shock, she almost instantly filled with water, and went to the bottom. A victualler, which lay alongside the *Royal George*, was swallowed up in the whirlpool, which the sudden plunge of so vast a body into the water occasioned; and several small craft, though at some moderate distance, were in imminent danger. The Admiral, with a number of officers and most of those who were between decks, perished. The greater part of those who were on the upper deck were saved by the boats of the fleet. The exact number of persons on board at the time could not be ascertained; but it was supposed that between 900 and 1,000 passed, with this awful suddenness into a future state, "with all their imperfections on their head." About 300 were saved.

On the glorious defeat of the French fleet, the first of June, 1794, Lord Howe with the fleet under his command, arrived at Spithead, and landed at Portsmouth on the 15th; and amidst the loudest acclamations, was conducted to the Governor's house on the grand parade. The following day, his Lordship had a levee, at which the Mayor, Aldermen and Burgesses were introduced, and presented an address to his Lordship. On the 25th, his Royal Highness Prince Ernest Augustus, and two of the young Princesses came here, went immediately to the Commissioner's house in the Dockyard, and there waited the coming of their Majesties, who arrived with the three other Princesses at the Commissioner's house about eleven o'clock the following day. The King, Queen, Prince and Princesses then proceeded in the royal barges to Spithead and went on board the Queen Charlotte, under a salute from the garrison, forts, and fleet. On their quitting the ship, they went round the fleet and then returned to the Commissioner's house.

On Friday the 27th, their Majesties had a levee at the Governor's house, where the Mayor, Aldermen and Burgesses were introduced to the King, and were most graciously received. They were afterwards introduced to the Queen.

On Saturday, the King, Queen and Royal Family witnessed the launch of the *Prince of Wales,* of 98 guns, then went in their barges on board the *Amphion* frigate at Spithead and returned in the evening under the same salutes as on the preceding days.

On Sunday, their Majesties and the Royal Family heard divine service at the Dock Chapel, afterwards went on board, and viewed the

Prince of Wales, then in a wet dock, and appeared highly gratified at
the exertions of the Artificers of the dock-yard in caulking and
coppering that ship, which went off the stocks at eleven o'clock on
Saturday morning, came into the wet dock on the next tide, and was
completely caulked and coppered in *nine* hours. In the evening, his
Majesty with Prince Ernest, walked round the fortifications of
Portsmouth, afterwards called at the Governor's house, where the
Queen and Princesses were on the balcony, with a band of music on
the green, and then returned to the Commissioner's about nine in the
evening.

On Monday morning, about nine o'clock, their Majesties and the
Royal Family left this town, and set sail for Southampton.

Earl St. Vincent, after having obtained a signal victory over the
French fleet, arrived at Spithead in August, 1799, and landed on the
18th at the Dock-yard; afterwards visited the town of Portsmouth,
and received the Mayor, Aldermen and Burgesses at the Admiral's
house in the High-street, and was by them admitted one of the
burgesses of the said town.

We shall now conclude our historical particulars respecting this
town with a brief, yet impartial recital of the visit the allied
sovereigns paid it in the year 1814.

On Wednesday the 22d of June, his Royal Highness the Prince
Regent, accompanied by his Royal Highness the Duke of Cambridge,
set out from Carlton-house and arrived at the Government-house,
Portsmouth, about four o'clock the same evening. On their arrival at
Portsdown Hill, they were received with a royal salute of 21 guns
from a brigade of Royal Artillery stationed at that point; at the same
time, also, a royal salute was fired from all the ships and vessels of
war lying at Spithead.

When his Royal Highness arrived at the Landport Gate, he was received by Lieutenant General Houstoun, Lieutenant-Governor of the Garrison, who presented his Royal Highness the keys of the town, which he immediately returned, and on his entrance was saluted with a triple discharge of all the artillery round the ramparts, and all the ships and vessels at Spithead fired a royal salute, and these salutes were repeated when his Royal Highness alighted from his carriage at the Governor's house.

The troops lined both sides of the road from the Government house to the Barracks at Hilsea, a distance of no less than three miles, and the roads, streets, ramparts and the Parade were thronged with spectators, who received his Royal Highness with the greatest demonstrations of loyalty and affection. His Royal Highness held a levee, and immediately after proceeded to the front of the Government-house, where he was received by the people with shouts and acclamations.

About half-past seven in the evening, his Majesty the King of Prussia, accompanied by their Royal Highnesses the Princes Royal, and William, Prince William, his Majesty's brother, and Prince Frederick of Prussia, and attended by Lord Charles Bentinck and several other persons of his Majesty's Court, were met without the town by a Guard of Honour which conducted the King of Prussia to the Lieut-Governor's house in St. Thomas's-street, which had been prepared for his Majesty's residence.

His Imperial Majesty, Alexander, Emperor of Russia, arrived about nine o'clock, accompanied by her Imperial Highness Catherine, Grand Duchess of Oldenburgh, and attended by the Earl of Yarmouth; Count Lieven, his Imperial Majesty's Ambassador, who proceeded to the Commissioner's house in the Dock-yard. By this time, the illuminations[70] had commenced, and presented a scene of

---

70 It would be injustice in us, if we were to omit describing the beautiful

grandeur and delight unknown to Portsmouth. Thousands paraded the streets inspecting the various exhibitions till a late hour, whom the fatigues of the day gradually dispersed, and the night passed off with the utmost order and regularity.

Thursday morning at ten o'clock his Royal Highness the Prince Regent together with the Dukes of York and Cambridge left the Government house in a coach and four, under a royal salute, and proceeded to the residence of the King of Prussia. His Majesty accompanied the Prince Regent in his carriage to the Dock yard where they were received by his Majesty the Emperor of Russia, from whence they proceeded through the Dock yard and embarked in a barge magnificently fitted up for their reception, in which the Royal Standard was immediately hoisted, and proceeded down the harbour to Spithead. Abreast of the Royal Barge on the right hand, a barge carried the Imperial Standard of Russia and another in the same situation on the left carried the Royal Standard of Prussia; both these

display the Government-house exhibited during the stay of the Royal Visitors. This building has a plain extensive front, with a balcony in the centre, supported by four neat columns: in front was the word "Peace," of an extensive size; on the outside were two brilliant stars; and outside these stars, rather above, the initials A. and F., supported by laurel. The balcony was decorated with festoons, and an imitation of drapery, the whole surmounted by a brilliant star and crown above each other. These various emblems were of very large dimensions, admirably formed, and expressed in coloured lamps. In addition to these, there were lamps in close double rows along the parapet of the building; and at a short distance below, as well as around the windows. The columns which supported the balcony, were likewise decorated with double rows of lamps, in a serpentine form; the whole producing a blaze of light and unity of design which astonished and attracted thousands, during the three nights it was exhibited. Indeed, no description can convey an idea any way equal to the splendour of the scene.

barges were filled with the suites of their respective sovereigns. The board of Admiralty with the Ambassadors of Austria and Russia and several other persons of distinction, in their barge bearing the Admiralty Flag, immediately preceded his Royal Highnesses barge. The barges of the Admirals and Captains carrying their respective flags followed in two lines according to their seniority.

As his Royal Highness passed the garrison, he was saluted with twenty one guns from the battery on the platform, and when the Royal Standard was seen from the fleet at Spithead, his Royal Highness was saluted in the same manner by the ships there, which was repeated by the guns on the platform; and as the royal party passed the ships, the yards were all manned and their crews gave three cheers. They then went on board the *Impregnable*, and the Royal Standard being hoisted, it was immediately saluted by the fleet and answered by a similar number of guns from the platform.

On the royal party leaving the *Impregnable,* a royal salute was again fired by the whole fleet. When the barges approached the shore at Southsea Castle, they were saluted by a *feu de joie* fired by the troops drawn up on Southsea Beach and from the battery on the platform. The Prince Regent, the King of Prussia and the Board of Admiralty landed at the Sally Port; but his Majesty the Emperor of Russia proceeded to the King's Stairs at the Dock-yard. His Royal Highness, accompanied by the King of Prussia, walked from the Sally Port to the Government house amidst the acclamations of thousands collected in the streets. In the evening the Prince Regent gave a dinner to the whole of the imperial-royal visitors, consisting of 120 covers of every delicacy of the season. While the company were at table, Marshal Blucher arrived at the Crown Inn, in a coach and four: the noble warrior was immediately introduced to the royal personages and received by them with the warmest congratulations.

Friday morning, his Royal Highness the Prince-Regent and the King and Princes of Prussia again went to Spithead, and during their absence the Emperor of Russia and the Grand Duchess of Oldenburgh, attended by Lord Viscount Melville, the Earl of Yarmouth, and the imperial suite, crossed over to Haslar Hospital; his Imperial Majesty after expressing the highest satisfaction at the general system of the Hospital returned with his suite to the Dock-yard.

The Prince Regent and King of Prussia having embarked, the procession moved nearly in the same order as the preceeding day to Spithead, and the royal party went on board the *Royal Soverign Yatch*[71] where the Royal Standard was hoisted. The fleet then got under weigh and proceeded to sea, and when his Royal Highness was at St. Helens he shifted his flag to and proceeded on board the *Impregnable* with the royal party. The fleet now under sail performed several evolutions and manoeuvered with the greatest celerity and precision, and then returned to Spithead, from whence they returned in the same way they did on the day before, to the Government-house, where they were received by Lord Bathurst and his Grace the Duke of Wellington, who had arrived (whilst his Royal Highness was on the water), in a coach and six; he was recognised by the people at the George Inn, and the horses being taken from his carriage, was drawn to the Government-house, amidst shouts of applause; when on the grand parade, the troops presented arms to his Grace, and during the time the music was playing "See the Conquering Hero comes," the troops and the immense assemblage of people rent the air with their acclamations. Soon after his entry into the Government-house, he came into the balcony to pay his respects to those who had so warmly welcomed him. When he made his

71[sic]

appearance an universal shout arose, the Cavalry whirled their sabres in the air, and thousands of voices exclaimed, "Long live Wellington." His Grace looked remarkably well, but rather thin, and much sunburnt. In the evening the Prince Regent gave a ball and supper at the Crown Inn, which was numerously attended, but his Royal Highness, was not present himself.

Saturday morning about nine o'clock, his Royal Highness held a levee at the Government-house, at which were present several military officers and the Mayor, Aldermen and Burgesses, who presented his Royal Highness an address; they were all most graciously received and his Royal Highness was pleased to confer the honour of knighthood on Henry White, Esquire, the mayor. This morning the Emperor of Russia and the King and Princes of Prussia honoured the Duke of Clarence with their presence to a breakfast at the Crown hotel. The Prince Regent left Portsmouth with their Imperial and Royal Majesties about ten o'clock in the morning. His Royal Highness after attending his friends along the coast, reached London on the 27th, gratified beyond measure with what he had seen during his excursion and the manner in which he and his friends had been received in Portsmouth.

Before his Royal Highness quitted the town he left £100 to the poor of the parishes of Portsmouth and Portsea; £50 to the poor of the parish of Gosport; £50 to the debtors in Portsmouth gaol; and £3000 to be distributed to the workmen of the Dock yard.

Thus closed a series of splendid scenes, which will be remembered and dwelt on with no common interest for years to come. The assembly of two foreign potentates, illustrious for their virtues — that of our own princes, statesmen and heroes — and lastly the assembly of those warriors who have been enabled by their own exertions to free their countries from slavery and despotism and give peace to

Europe — this l say, is not an every day's occurrence. The interest of the scene is fully exemplified by the thousands who flocked from all parts of the kingdom. We have endeavoured in the foregoing pages to attempt to convey some idea of the magnificence and grandeur of the scene, but our description must only be considered as a rough outline, the recollection of those who were present can alone finish the *picture!*

CHAPTER II

The Borough of Portsmouth.

NOTWITHSTANDING many eminent writers have written on the origin and constitution of boroughs, yet the period when their representatives were first admitted into the National Council is by no means clearly ascertained. It is, however, very evident cities and towns sent members to Parliament as early as the twenty third year of Edward I[72].

---

72 Dr Brady produces authorities to show that Cities and Boroughs did not send members till the 23d of Edward I. This difference between Prynne and Brady may nevertheless be accommodated: for, as Hume observes, the former precedent of representatives for the boroughs summoned by the Earl of Leicester was regarded as the act of a violent usurpation, and had been discontinued in all the subsequent Parliaments. He therefore considers the 23d of Edward I as the real and true epoch of the House of Commons. The same historian adds that the clergy scrupled to meet on the king's writ, lest by such obedience they should seem to acknowledge the authority of a temporal power; but that at length a compromise took place, by which the king was to issue this writ to the archbishop, and he in consequence to summon his clergy, who now hesitated no longer to meet in convocation. This expedient was the cause why the ecclesiastics met in two houses of convocation under their archbishops, and formed not one estate, as in other countries of Europe, which was the king's first intention. The summons directed to the Archbishop of Canterbury for convening his clergy, as it will illustrate and confirm what I have advanced, is inserted at No. IV. Brady in his Treatise on Boroughs, cites various Records to show that the king's tenants in demesne deliberated *separately* from the knights and burgesses, and generally taxed themselves in a proportion higher by *one-third* than the rest of the Laity. WORSELEY'S ISLE OF WIGHT [Edward 1 came to power

The principal cause of burgesses being summoned to parliament was to give their consent to taxes propounded to, or imposed on them; previous to this reign, they had been *talliated* or paid *tallage*, according to the imposition on them, or acceptance of what they offered by the king's officers or justices.

The first charter of immunities granted to this town was from King Richard I, dated the 2nd of May, 1194, by which he granted a fair or mart for 15 days to begin on the feast of St. Peter, a weekly market on Thursday, and various other immunities.

This charter of Richard I is similar to most of those given at that early period; the names of the witnesses are given below[73].

King John, by charter dated the 25th of October, 1200, granted to the Borough of Portsmouth, the same privileges they enjoyed before under the charter of King Richard his brother, with this exception, however, towards the end; *"Et phibemus ne quis eos disturbet in aliq° sup foisf'turam nostra' sicut carta Regis Rici fratris nostri racionabiliter testatur except h° quod additur in clausula ubi dicitur i carta Regis Ricardi no ponantur in plitum de aliq° tenemeto eiusdm ville nisi coram nobis ibi nos aposuimus vl capitali Justic?"*[74]

---

in 1272. His 23rd year is 1294-5]

73	Willmus de ecclia	Robertus filius Rogi
	- sce marie	Ganfr' de say
	Mager Phus.	Willmus de Stagno
	Ganfr' fil' petri.	Willmus Mallum

74 [This note appears in *Extracts From Records In The Possession Of The Municipal Corporation Of The Borough Of Portsmouth*, 1891. "King John granted a Charter of the 5th October, in the second year of his reign. This varies from the Charter of Richard merely by enlarging the exception as to pleas concerning tenements in the town. The clause in John's Charter excepts pleas before the king himself or his chief justice."]

A.D 1230, another charter was granted by his successor Henry III, in which he confirmed *"hominibz. nostris de Portesmuth[75]"* the preceding charters of King Richard, and King John.

Portsmouth in 1255 received a second charter from Henry III, being nothing more than a confirmation of former grants.

In the following year this monarch granted another to this borough, in which he gave *"'probis hominibz nostris" to our honest men* of Portesmuth a *Gild of Merchants*, and many other additional and important privileges, not before enjoyed.

In all probability this town was now increasing considerably in trade and importance, for it was considered at this period a great privilege to have a *Gilda Mercatoria*, and indeed sometimes afforded a *livelihood* to a Member or Burgess of the *Gild of Merchants*; for wherever such a Burgess resided, he had many important privileges attached to the office and place of such community or fraternity.

As a further proof of what I have already advanced, the *men of Portesmuth*, in the reign of this king, petitioned Henry III that he would allow none of the Justices that went their circuits in *Hantshire* to come to their town and hold the pleas of the town of Portsmouth, which ought to be brought before the Justices according to the charter of King Richard I, which was granted them on the payment of *three casks of wine.*[76]

This Borough first sent two burgesses to parliament in the year 1298, the 26th of Edward I.

---

75 ["Our men of Portsmouth"]

76 Homines de Portesmuth debent tres dolia vini, ut Rex præcipiat quosdam ex Justiciarus Itinerantibus in comitatu Suhantoniæ mitti usque Portesmuth, ad tenendum ibi placita illius villæ quæ ad Justiciarios pertinent, secundum tenorem cartae Regis Ricardi avunculi Regis.

MAG. ROT. 3 HEN. III. ROT. 3, a.

In the second year of Edward II[77], writs were, according to Prynne, directed to the Bailiffs of the Town of Portsmouth, of the Town of Southampton, of the Isle of Wight, Christ Church, Andover, Basingstoke, Odiam and Aton, but those Bailiffs made no returns to the Sheriff. In the fourth year of Edward II, other writs were directed to the Bailiffs of the *Town of Portsmouth* and several other towns, but no returns were made of them.[78]

At this period Sheriffs and Bailiffs were extremely negligent in returning writs to parliament. But it appears that the cause was chiefly owing to the poverty of the boroughs; for although the town of Portsmouth exerted itself so in the former reign, as to have pleas held within its walls, yet we must necessarily conclude that it was far from being in an opulent condition in the reign of Edward II. Indeed, it must have been so poor as to have been unable to pay the burgesses their expenses or wages during the sitting of parliament.

One principal reason of the poverty of our ancient boroughs was the heavy taxes and tallages imposed on them by the king; for there were two chief taxors appointed by him in every county, who elected twelve in every hundred to raise every man's personal estate according to the true value, and then to levy a thirtieth or an eighteenth part of it, as it was granted by the earls, barons, knights, &c in parliament. They also appointed such and as many as they thought fit in every city, town, or borough to inquire into every man's personal estate in those places, and find out the true value of it, and then to levy a twentieth or twelfth part thereof, as it had been granted by the citizens, burgesses, and tenants of the king's ancient demesnes in parliament. And that they might tax and value every man's estate truly and really, the taxors were sworn not to do otherwise for love,

---

77 [Edward II assumed the throne in 1307]

78 Prynne's Brev. Parl. p.295

hatred, favour, gift, or otherwise.

In the eighth year of Edward III[79], this mode of taxation was altered, upon the barons, knights, citizens, and burgesses complaining to the king in parliament that the taxors and collectors for bribes spared some men and by colour of their office extorted from others more than they ought to pay and applied it to their own use. Accordingly, commissioners were sent into every county in England to agree and compound with the inhabitants of every town that was to pay a fifteenth, and also with the communities and corporations of cities and boroughs, which paid a tenth for the sums they were to pay. The sum fixed upon the particular towns, cities, and boroughs were for the future collected and rated most commonly by the inhabitants themselves.

The *town of Portsmouth* was, in the 15th year of Edward III seized into the King's hands for not accounting to the King; and it was commanded that the town of Portsmouth should not be permitted to have return of writs and summonses because they came not, nor sent upon the Sheriff's last account, to answer to the King for the levyable debts within the town and liberties. The Corporation of the town, alarmed at this rigorous measure of the King's, sent one of their Bailiffs to him, who entreated that he would be pleased to admit them to fine, which after some persuasion he was permitted to do, and paid to the King a fine of *half a mark*, for having their privileges restored them.

King Edward II, by letters patent, bearing date from *Wyndesore*, the 12th of February, A.D. 1313, confirmed and ratified the preceding charters of Richard and John; as did likewise Edward III in 1359; Richard II in 1385 ; Edward IV in 1463; and Richard III in 1484.

It was the policy of Queen Elizabeth to favour and promote the

---

79 [Edward III assumed the throne in 1327]

power and importance of Corporations in order to counterpoise the influence of the nobility in the state; and by that means shelter the crown from danger in that quarter. Letters Patent and Charters of Incorporation were accordingly granted to several places in the kingdom; and many boroughs which had not before enjoyed that privilege were summoned to send representatives to the Commons House of Parliament.

Queen Elizabeth, in 1600, after setting forth in her grant or charter that the Borough of Portsmouth was then governed by a Mayor, two Bailiffs, two Constables and other public officers and had been so time immemorial, gave the Corporation a power of electing Justices of the Peace, a privilege they had never enjoyed before; and appointed the Corporate Body to be stiled by the name of *Mayor and Burgesses*.

This charter remained in full forced till the year 1627, when Charles I, after reciting in his grant that the Borough of Portsmouth in the county of Southampton is an ancient Borough, and the Burgesses, Freemen, and Inhabitants thereof, sometimes called by the name of the *Honest Men of Portsmouth*; sometimes by the name of the *Portsmouth Burgesses,* sometimes by the name of the *Men of Portsmouth*, sometimes by the name of the *Burgesses of Portsmouth,* and afterwards by the name of the *Mayor and Burgesses* of the Borough of Portsmouth, directed they should be called and known by the name of the *Mayor, Aldermen, and Burgesses*, (the name they at present are stiled) and have a common seal; make bye-laws; impose fines; have power to make a Deputy Mayor; to hold a *Court of Record* every week except the week of *Easter, Whitsuntide* and the *birth of our Saviour Jesus Christ*, to be held before the Mayor or Recorder, and four Aldermen; to hold a *Court Leet*, and *view of Frank pledge* twice a year; to *elect* Justices of

the Peace; to have a prison or jail; to have a Town Clerk, who is to be
Clerk of the Market; to have power to chuse two Serjeants at Mace;
the Mayor to have the goods and chattels of felons; to be free of toll;
the *Inhabitants* not to be *summoned* to Assizes or Sessions at
Winchester; to have a Guild of Merchants; to have a fair at St. Peter's
day for fourteen days; to have the *power to weave broad cloth and
kerseys*[80]; to hold manors, messuages and lands; to pay the annual
rent of £12. 10s 6d into the Exchequer, and enjoy all the privileges
and liberties of preceding Charters or Letters of Incorporation.

Although this is the charter they are at present governed by, yet
Charles II in 1682 granted another, in which the Town of Gosport is
considered and made a part of the Corporation. In the latter end of
this reign, the Borough of Portsmouth, following the example of
many others in the kingdom, surrendered the charter of Charles I,
and accepted another from King Charles II, under which they acted
till the abdication of James II in 1688, when it was discovered by
Colonel Kingsley (then Member for Portsmouth) that the charter of
Charles I was in the hands of a Mr. Giogne, that it had not been duly
surrendered nor any enrolment made of it, and he, on application
from the Corporation, procured them the charter from Mr. Giogne,
by which means that of Charles II became void, the Corporation
claiming nothing from it, unless it is the wearing of scarlet gowns,
which the Mayor and Aldermen do to this day.

This recovery of the charter of Charles I was a circumstance
highly favourable to the freedom of this borough, since by that of his
successor, the Mayor, Aldermen, Recorder, Justices, Burgesses and
Town Clerk were removable, from time to time, at the will of the
crown.

In the year 1689, March 24th, a petition was presented to the

---

80 [A form of coarse woven cloth]

House of Commons by Henry Slingsby, Esq. showing that Nicholas Hedger, Mayor of this borough, upon pretence of having surrendered his office, did by undue means cause himself to be returned, notwithstanding he is still the legal Mayor. Upon this petition no report appears on the books of the House.

In the year 1695, divers inhabitants of this town, paying scot and lot and having a right to vote, stated in a petition to the House that they were precluded and prevented from voting for Edmund Dummer, Esq. by many *illegal* practices on the part of *Nicholas Hedger*, Mayor of this borough, viz. by shutting the gates of the town to prevent those voting who lived without, and by threatening many of the townsmen with corporal punishment for offering to poll for Mr. Dummer, and also in an hostile manner, by keeping a GUARD OF SOLDIERS to *threaten and discourage* Mr. Dummer's friends from voting for him, by which, and many other *flagrant* and *unconstitutional* practices, the said *Mayor* got himself returned.

On December 28th, 1695, Matthew Aylmer, Esq, petitioned against the return of Colonel Gibson, by reason of the Mayor having, at a private consultation with a few Aldermen, put the common seal to an indenture and return in manifest wrong to the petitioner, who had the majority of votes.

The House of Commons resolved, *"That the right of election for Burgesses to serve in Parliament for this Borough, is in the Mayor, Aldermen, and Burgesses of the said Borough* ONLY.

"That John Gibson and Mathew Aylmer Esqs are not duly elected for this Borough.

"That the said election of Burgesses for this Borough, is a *void election."*

These resolutions being read twice, were agreed to by the house.

On February 3d 1710, it was resolved by the House, "That *Joseph*

Whitehorn, Esq, who was elected Mayor of the Borough of Portesmouth, on the 10th of December, 1709, and had not duly qualified himself for that office, according to law, by taking the *Sacrament* of the *Lord's Supper*, according to the rites of the Church of England, *within* one year next before the election, was *not legal* Mayor of the said Borough."

Resolved: "That the Aldermen elected during the said pretended mayoralty of the said Mr. Whitehorn, are not *legal* Aldermen; and the *Burgesses* elected during his *pretended* mayoralty, have *not* a right to vote in the election for members to serve in Parliament for the said Borough of Portsmouth."

On December 1st 1710, was presented a petition of Sir William Giffard and Sir James Wishart, Knts, against the *illegal* return of Sir John Jennings and Sir Charles Wager, the *pretended* Mayor, *Henry Seager* Esq and Thomas Ridge and James White Esqs, and several others who acted and voted as Aldermen, though neither of them had *taken* the *Sacrament* and the necessary *oaths*, as prescribed by Act of Parliament, besides using many other *indirect* practices in procuring votes.

Resolved: "That Sir Charles Wager and Sir John Jennings, are *not duly elected for this Borough.*

"That Sir James Wishart and Sir William Giffard Knts, are *duly elected* for this Borough."

Portsmouth, in the year 1714, presented the following address by Captain Henry Stanyford and Mr. Thomas Blackley against the Harleian ministry; they were introduced to King George I by his Grace the Duke of Marlborough, and had the honour of kissing his Majesty's hand :—

"We heard the memory of our Great Deliverer reviled, his glorious undertaking disparag'd and reproached; and principles advanc'd, and countenanced by persons work'd into power, that overturned your right to your dominions. We saw the advantages gain'd by the most glorious and successful war, thrown up at once by an *Inglorious Peace*, faithful Allies deserted, the solemn faith of nations ridicul'd, and conquerors made to stoop at the demands of those whom they had overcome. We beheld our trade in the most valuable branches neglected; the avow'd enemies of your title conniv'd at, caress'd, advanc'd, and the most zealous friends to your accession reproached as enemies to your immediate predecessor, and removed from honourable posts and offices; and violent persecutions commenced and carry'd on against those members of corporate bodies, that were most hearty in your interests; and the authority and treasure of the nation abus'd and misapply'd to crush your friends: But, in the critical juncture, God was pleased to send your Majesty to scatter our fears. Under your just and wise administration, we assure ourselves of the redress of every grievance, and that the nation's honour will be carry'd, to it's utmost height. On such a prospect, allow us *Mighty Prince* to confess our joy unutterable."

In the year 1774, an information in the nature of a Quo Warranto was issued against Sir John Carter, to show by what authority he claimed to exercise the office of a Burgess of this borough.

The information alledged that this office and franchise of a burgess has been, and still is, a place of great trust and pre-eminence within the said borough, touching the rule and government of the said town. That within the said borough there have been, and now ought to be, an *indefinite number of burgesses*. That by the charter of 3 Charles I, the mayor, aldermen and burgesses were incorporated under the name and title of Mayor, Aldermen and Burgesses of the Borough of Portsmouth. That the charter nominated the first Mayor and twelve persons to be Aldermen, and then grants, "that it should and might be lawful for the Mayor and Aldermen, &c, or the major part of them, from time to time, and at all times then after for ever, when, and as often as it should appear to them to be fit and necessary, to name so many and such persons to be Burgesses as they should please, and to the said Burgesses so chosen, to administer an oath for their faithfully executing the said office of Burgess." That this charter was accepted by the then mayor and burgesses of the said borough and that the defendant on the 18th day of May, 1751, was elected by the *major part* of the mayor and aldermen; and that *before* he took upon himself to exercise the place, office and franchize of such Burgess he was duly sworn, according to the usage of the said Borough, into the said office.

The replication set forth other parts of the Charter, which gave the corporation a power to take lands and make bye-laws; and then stated that the Mayor, Aldermen, and Burgesses, or the major part of them, from time to time should have power to assemble themselves annually, every *Monday* seven night before the feast of St. Michael the Archangel, and name one of the Aldermen to be Mayor. That a Court of Record was appointed by the said Charter to be held before the Mayor, Recorder, and Aldermen, or any four of them; and also a Court Leet to be held before the Mayor, Recorder, and Aldermen. And that the Mayor and Recorder, and every Mayor for one year after his mayoralty, and three of the Aldermen, to be chosen as aforesaid, should be justices of the said Borough. That lastly a court of *oyer* and *terminer* was also appointed by the said charter to be held by the Mayor, Recorder and three Aldermen.

After much debate by the counsel on both sides, Chief Justice Ashhurst gave it as his opinion that judgment ought to be for the king in as much as the Burgess on his election into that office was only of the age of *five years* and ten months, for the power which the charter gives of electing Burgesses in this borough is to be exercised when and as often as it shall appear to the Mayor, Aldermen, and Burgesses to be *fit* and *necessary*. By that it meant, fit and necessary for the present purposes of the Corporation; and the persons intended, such as are capable of taking upon themselves the immediate execution of the office; not persons to be nominated only, and who might or might not act, or be capable of acting in future, as circumstances and events might turn out.

The right of election in this town, having, as before observed, been determined by the House of Commons to be *exclusively* in the Corporation, the same *influence* prevailed here, for a number of years, as at Plymouth: and the admiralty had ever been permitted to have the nomination of its members. The Corporation however (principally composed of men of independent fortunes, and averse to the war with America, and Lord North's administration), refused to accept the ministerial nomination of Peter Taylor, Esq, the Army Commissary, upon the death of the late Sir Matthew Featherstonhaugh, in 1774, and invited Joshua Iremonger of Wherewell, in this county, to oppose the interest of Government. But as the *patriotic* party had not yet acquired sufficient strength to overcome that influence which had usually prevailed here, Mr. Taylor carried his election by a majority of votes.

Government was so irritated at this opposition on the part of the Corporation that the ensuing year it moved the Court of King's Bench for informations in the nature of *Quo Warranto* against the Mayor, several of the Aldermen, and *sixty three* of the Burgesses. These informations having been severally obtained, and trials had thereon, judgment of ouster was obtained against the whole number. Similar informations were then moved on behalf of the *Patriotic* party against the ministerial party, and twenty nine of the latter were likewise ousted. These judgments left the corporation *without* a Mayor or Recorder, only four Aldermen remained in their office, and a *few* of the Burgesses.

Administration now had so far succeeded as to have a *clear majority* in this GARBLED CORPORATION; but of the four remaining Aldermen, William Carter senior Esq, Mr. White, Mr. Linzee, and Mr. Varloe, the two former being in the independent interest, and the two latter in that of Government; and as the power of making Aldermen and nominating candidates for the office of Mayor is vested by the *bye laws* of the corporation in the *Court of Aldermen*, no election could legally be made for either.

Notwithstanding this impediment, the majority of Burgesses who were in the interest of Government, however, assembled, and *assuming* to themselves a *power of chusing* a MAYOR, elected a *Mr. Monday*, an officer of the customs in this port, and one of the Burgesses, into that office. This election being *illegal*, judgment of *ouster* was soon obtained against him; but the Burgesses still persevering in the same mode of election, as soon as judgment of ouster was declared against one, set about electing another of their own party, and continued this practice for the space of nearly NINE YEARS; at the expiration of which time, *Linzee* and *Varloe*, the two *ministerial* Aldermen died and left the corporate power in the hands of their opponents; the *Earl of Sandwich* also, who had been considered the *patron* and *supporter* of the Ministerial interest in this Borough, being at this time removed from the office of first Lord of the Admiralty, they lost that support by which they had been enabled for so many years to carry on their opposition.

Messrs *Carter* and *White*, the two only remaining Aldermen, having now the *sole command* of the *Corporation,* and the election of Mayor of necessity falling upon one of them, Mr. Carter was accordingly chosen on the Michaelmas-day following. And the Corporation having once more obtained a legal form, a Court of Aldermen was held, the vacancies were filled up, and a number of new Burgesses elected.

On the 7th of August, 1800, in the mayoralty of the late *William Goldson*, Esq, the Mayor, Aldermen and Burgesses, attended by several officers of this borough, went the *water boundaries*[81] at high

---

81 The following are the *land bounds* of this borough, taken in the year 1727.

"First ride three times round, the Market-house, then through the Sally Port to the water's edge, to the lower end of the Point: then through *Smock Alley* [now East Street on Point], and over Town Quay, and so to the Gun wharf, and round it; from thence to the Dock, and round it, and round the jetty heads, to the further end of the wall by the boat-houses, where was formerly a door, and somebody must be put there over the wall. Then keep as close to the wall as possible, till you come out of the Dock Gates; then go on the outside of the wall to the back of the same wall, where was formerly a door; then round Fenning's Marsh, all along shore to Whale Island, and round the Island, then round all the points at Stamshaw and Tipner; then along shore till you come to the outside of the Vicarage Field, now in possession of *Mr. Ridge*; then enter a ditch of a field of *Mr. Brouncher's*, now in possession of *Doctor Brady*; then come out at a gate opposite to the bound stone, to the northward of the Green Post; then turn *three* times round the stone, and *three* times round the post; then to the ditch at the south corner from Green Post, and so keep in a strait line till you come to George Ridge's smith's shop, at Stubbington; then turn up to Stubbington House, go through part of the garden, and part of Stubbington farm-house; then to a gate leading to *Bewston's Field*; then enter the field, and keep close to the hedge on the left hand, till you come to the lane that leads to Kingston Church, and so round the bound stone in Kingston pond, *three times*; then go northward to Lake Lane, and down Lake Lane, till you come to *Beeston's*

water, in the following procession, the Aldermen being in their scarlet gowns, and the Burgesses in their black. In the first boat, having a blue flag with the half moon and star (the arms of the Corporation) in yellow, the Harbour Master accompanied by a Serjeant at Mace, bearing the *little mace*; in the second boat, a band of music; in the third boat, the Mayor and Aldermen, attended by the Town Clerk, a Sergeant at Mace, bearing the mace, and the Cryer,

---

Field, adjoining the Common Field; then through the gate, keeping close to the hedge on the left hand, till you enter the ditch into Kingston Church Common Field, and keep close by the hedge on the gate, till you come to the land, late *James White's*; then close by the hedge to the Field of *Robert Grigg*, late *Mounsher's* and so to Wish Lane, and then to the Gibbet. Somebody must ride through the ditch that parts *Cozens's* land from *Mr. Belfield's*, and the Morass, or as nigh as they can; then three times round the Gibbet (the Gibbet of *Felton*, who assassinated the Duke of Buckingham in the High-street of this town in 1623 – see earlier account) then along shore to the Sally Port, from thence up Street, and *three times* round the Markethouse, which finishes the circuit."

Having thus described the *land bounds* of this borough, we here subjoin those of the *parish* of Portsmouth, as perambulated on September the 2nd, A.D. 1813.

The Boundary of the Parish of Portsmouth commences at low water mark, about 100 paces to the south-east of the Hot Walls; thence proceed in a northerly direction till you get into the large Moat; cross the little Moat, keeping close to the right hand wall of the large Moat, till you arrive at the small spur leading to Landport Bridge; there cross the Moat again, and proceed along the outer wall to Landport Bridge, thence along the Moat, keeping always close to the outer wall, to nearly opposite the angle formed by the line from Quay Gate; cross the road (by permission) to the King's Mill; keep close to the Mill, and follow that line to the bastion at Mill Gate; mount the bastion, and descend on the opposite side, close to the portcullis; then

supported by a boat on each side, with constables. In four boats following, the Burgesses, supported by a boat on each side and followed by other boats with other officers of the borough.

The Procession left the Old Sally Port at 10 in the morning and went along under the platform, as near to the bound post on Southsea beach as the water would admit of, and from thence in a direct line across to the end of Green Lane, or as near to it as the tide would admit; then returned along the shore to the harbour near Blockhouse-point, rounding a little into Haslar Lake and on to the Hard at Gosport beach, where the Serjeant at Mace touched the Hard with one oar, and the Town Clerk claimed jurisdiction in the following words: *"I claim jurisdiction here for the Mayor of Portsmouth, and by his direction, on behalf of himself, the Aldermen and Burgesses thereof, in as full and ample a manner as was ever claimed and enjoyed by any of the Mayors, his predecessors."*

From Gosport Beach it was intended that the first boat should

---

from the portcullis in a direct line (intersecting obliquely the foot bridge and water) to the centre of the Gun-wharf's large gates; thence in a direct line to the Store-keeper's house, half way through the house, up three steps to the left; proceed on that line; descend three steps to the right, and follow the course of the entry to the garden fence; thence to a pear tree in the first Clerk's garden, thence in a line to a small chimney on Mr. Spencer's laundry; thence to that angle of the wall of the Gun wharf, touching the Common Hard; and thence all along the harbour line, and cross over to the point from the nearest angle. From the left hand of Spring Street, or on an angle to No. 7, on the opposite side, through the centre of No. 7, to Martyr Yard, in Fountain Street; then in a line intersecting the chimneys of the two lines of the houses, strait on by the Infirmary, including the whole of the water course to the Weigh-bridge - and from the corner of Halfway House, to the corner of the Weigh-bridge House, including the waste land formed by the angle.

have gone up to Forton Mill-dam, between Barrow Castle and Weovil, and there claim jurisdiction, but the tide not serving, the procession proceeded on to Hardway and Bedneham Creek, which the first boat entered, and immediately returned, and on resuming its former situation the whole went to Fareham Quay. The first boat went up the river to the Fareham Mill-dam, at which place the Serjeant laid an oar on the bridge at the head of the dam and again claimed jurisdiction in the manner before described.

The rest of the procession waited on the latter quay and were joined by the first boat, when the whole returned down the lake to Wicker Hard, there the first boat left the others and proceeded to Porchester, and from thence along the shore to Pauls-grove and Wymering, where jurisdiction was likewise claimed by the Serjeant in the same manner; from thence round Horsea Island to Tipner, back to the *Laurel* frigate lying in the harbour, to which place the rest of the procession had immediately gone from Fareham Lake, and where an elegant dinner was provided by the direction of the Mayor.

From the circumstance of the insufficiency of water not permitting the procession to go to some particular places within the boundaries, the Mayor, with Stephen Gaselee Esq, one of the Aldermen, in their scarlet gowns, attended by Mr. Pink, as Serjeant at Mace, in his black gown, and Mr Battershell, harbour master, went in a boat before high water, with the *Corporation colours* flying from the Bathing-house on the Point Beach, to Forton Mill round Barrow Castle, along the Gosport shore and Docks, to the southward to Haslar Lake and through Forbe's Bridge to Stoke Causeway, from thence returning and went up the other branch of the lake to the bridge erecting over it, for the new Parish Poor House building on Ewer Common. Proclamation was made by the Mayor at the Dam, at Forton Mill, at White and Parmeter's Docks, Page's Wharfs, Forbe's

Bridge and at Stoke Causeway to support the jurisdiction; and from thence the procession immediately returned, and landed at Point Beach.

CHAPTER III
The Town of Portsmouth.

PORTSMOUTH is situated on the Island of Portsea, which is about sixteen miles in circumference. This part of the country lies low, and appears to have been gradually gained from the sea, or from the effect of some extraordinary convulsion of nature that might have probably at the same time separated the Isle of Wight from the main land of Hampshire.

This town is bounded on the North by a range of heights called *Portsdown*; on the south by Spithead, and the Isle of Wight; on the East by Hayling Island, and on the West by the harbour and the Town of Gosport. From its being thus eligibly situated, it is not only completely sheltered from the bleak winds, but open at the same time to receive the genial and refreshing breezes from the sea; from which circumstance its situation for health must be equal, if not superior, to many other towns in the kingdom.

The markets also in this place are well supplied with butcher's meat, poultry, and every kind of salt-water fish; and few markets can boast of such quantities of excellent vegetables as are brought to this, and it must be also remarked that the broccoli sold here is allowed to be the best in the kingdom. The market days are Tuesday, Thursday, and Saturday.

In the year 1768 an Act of Parliament was obtained for lighting, watching and paving the Town of Portsmouth, and paving was completed in 1773 at the expence of nearly £9000, and it has since received considerable improvements from the pulling down the old edifices and removing nuisances and obstructions, so as now to render it one of the cleanest, handsomest and most regular borough towns in the kingdom.

The Town of Portsmouth consists of four principal streets, running parallel to each other, intersected at right angles by others of less magnitude. The first that appears, after having entered through the Landport gate, is the High street, which is very broad and regular, and what greatly adds to its beauty is its curving situation, being almost similar in appearance to a bow.

The grand Parade situated at the lower end of the High street is so spacious that two regiments of soldiers may be reviewed on it with ease. On the North side are a row of elegant buildings, and on the opposite side stands the main guard-house, belonging to the garrison.

Towards the upper end of the grand Parade stands a fine old building, called the Government-house, which originally formed part of a *"faire hospitale"* or *Domus Dei* founded for twelve old men by *Peter de Rupibus*, Bishop of Winchester. It, however, displays now but little of its monastic origin, the alterations in it having been great and frequent.

During the reign of King John many controversies and disputes arose between the Prior of this Hospital and the Prior of Southwick, which were finally settled in the year 1229, as appears from a copy of an old MS[82] in my possession, on condition that the master and brothers of God's house should acceed to the following regulations.

1st. The said prior and convent agreed that divine service might be celebrated in the said hospital by two priests.

2nd. That it was lawful for any foreign priest to do so, who might come there for the sake of seeing a kinsman or relation.

3rd. That they may have two bells not exceeding the weight of the bells belonging to the Mother Church, which might ring at Matins,

---

82 [Manuscript]

Vespers and for the dead.

4th. That after the bells of the *new* Mother Church have rung, the said brothers shall receive none of the parishioners of *Portesmuth* to confession, nor to the Communion of Christ's Body, unless he happen to be sick, and wishes particularly for a priest from the Hospital, in that case, he shall not be denied confession, the Parish Priest having first given his consent.

5th. That they shall not receive any stranger to confession *publickly* during the forty days in Lent, unless the brothers, sisters and sick, lying then at the Hospital. Nevertheless if any stranger shall seek advice of any priest belonging to the Hospital, it shall be lawful for him to receive him *privately*.

6th. That the brothers of the Hospital shall not receive any of the parishioners on the *eight* chief feasts, viz. the birth day of our Lord, the Epiphany, the Purification, the Assumption of the Blessed Mary, the Ascension of our Lord, the Nativity of the Blessed Mary, and the Feast of Aill Saints. But if it shall happen that any of the said parishioners of *Portesmuth* shall come to hear divine service on the said eight Festivals or Sundays, they may be admitted and their *offering* (if they shall make any) shall be wholly and entirely restored to the Mother Church under the penalty here under expressed, unless the said parishioners shall on the said days, make satisfaction to the Mother Church.

7th. That it shall be lawful for any belonging to the Hospital to enter ships, or give blessings, read the gospel, or beg alms after having read it.

8th. That the said Hospital may have a cemetery as well for the brothers and sisters of the said Hospital, as for families and sick persons dying there.

That if any stranger shall chuse to be interred at the Hospital, it is lawful for them to receive him provided his body shall have been *first* carried to the Mother Church and mass celebrated there.

9th. That the parishioners of *Portesmuth* ought to leave their *first* legacy to the Mother Church.

10th. That the said brothers of the Hospital shall pay yearly for ever to the Mother Church the sum of twenty shillings.

11th. And for the greater security of these articles the said brothers, having taken their corporal oaths on the Holy Evangelists, bound themselves under the penalty of *40 shillings* to be paid to the said prior and Convent of *Suwicke*[83] to observe faithfully the whole of them.

From the register of *William of Wykeham*, it appears that a brother of his was prebendary of *Mapledurham* in the church of Boreham in 1370; Archdeacon of Winchester in 1372; which having resigned, he became Archdeacon of Wilts in 1382; and *Warden* of the *Hospital of St. Nicholas* at Portsmouth on the death of Richard Wykeham in 1378. This hospital was situated near the gate of the chapel belonging to God's House.

On the suppression of the order of the knight's Templars, *Uggeton,* a manor in the Isle of Wight, which had been presented to them by *Mascarell,* Lord of Brooke, was given to God's House of Portsmouth[84].

---

83 [Southwick]

84 By a deed dated 1272, from *Richard le Conceror* of *Portesmue,* to God and the Church of the blessed Mary of *Suwyk,* the brothers of God's House for a piece of land granted to the said convent received yearly *three silver pennies,* paid on the feast of St. Michael for ever.

Also by a deed in 1276, from *Robert de Sanctus Dionysius* of *Portesmue* to *Ada de Stobitone,* the said brothers received for a house and its appurtenances, situate in the *High street* of the Town of *Portesmue, four*

At the dissolution of religious houses by Henry VIII, it was converted into a dwelling-house for the residence of the governor of this town, since which period great alterations and modern improvements have been made in it. The annual revenues of this house were at the dissolution valued at £33 19s 5 ¼d.

That part of the parade which fronts this building was formerly the ancient cemetery belonging to the hospital; a few years since

---

silver shillings every year for ever, to be paid on the feast of St. Michael, and the blessed John the Baptist.

On the death of the celebrated *William of Wykeham* he left the following legacy in his will:—

"Item lego Hospitali Sancti Nicholai de Portesmuth vnam par vestimentorum, cum calice."

Fearful of extending our Appendix to too large a bulk we have inserted below a list of the quantity of land belonging to the Hospital of *Domus Dei*, in the several furlongs and common fields of Portsmouth as taken in the reign of Queen Elizabeth.

Catelife Furlonge God's house Portesmuth	iii	di Aker.
Chilmer Furlonge (North) ditto	i	Stich.
Black Thorne Furlonge (South) ditto.............		di Aker
God's House Furlonge (North) ditto.............	vi	Akers.
Full Sea Furlonge (West) ditto.............		di Aker
Foutorne Furlonge (West) ditto.............	i	Aker.
Wett Furlonge (East) ditto.............	iii	Akers.
Water Furlonge (West) ditto	iii	di Akers.
Peckshall Furlonge (West) ditto.............	vi	Akers.
Kingwelrose Furlonge (West) ditto.............	i	Aker.
Newgate Furlonge (North to ye Railes) do.....	i	di Aker.
Short Broome Furlonge (South) ditto		di Aker.
Mill Stile Furlonge (West) ditto		di Aker.
St. Andrew Furlonge (East) ditto.............	viii	di Akers,

some workmen being employed to lay a foundation for the erection of new works, they dug up a vast number of human sculls and bones which had been interred there many hundred years prior to the circumstance of their discovery.

Near this hospital is the ancient chapel belonging to it, which has been repaired of late years and assigned to the use of the officers and soldiers of the garrison. It was *here* that Charles II was married to Catherine, Infanta of Portugal, on May 22nd 1662, by Dr. Sheldon, Lord Bishop of London, in the presence of many of the nobility of both kingdoms.

The Governor's house, during the existence of this Monastery, was a large square stone building at the bottom of and facing the High-street; which for some time after the removal of the Governor was used as a magazine for powder, but another having been erected

Shovell Furlonge (West) ditto.............		di Akers
Lake Furlonge (East) ditto.............	vii	di Akers.
Kingwell Furlonge (North) ditto.............	iii	Akers.
Close Furlonge (East) ditto.............		di Aker.
Reddish Furlonge (North).............		di Aker.
Gore Furlonge (South) ditto.............	i	di Aker.
Lake Furlonge (West) ditto.............	v	di Akers.
Pease Furlonge (West) ditto.............	ii	Akers.
Copner Furlonge (South) ditto.............		di Aker.
Bramble Furlonge (West) ditto	ii	di Akers.
Stobington Furlonge (North) ditto.............	i	di Aker.
North Streete Furlonge (North) ditto.............	ii	Akers.
South Streete Furlonge (North) ditto.............	iii	di Akers.
Abram Furlonge (West) ditto.............	i	di Aker.
White bedde Furlonge (West) ditto.............	i	Aker.
Curges Crofte, ditto.............	i	di Aker.
Totals	Ixx	Akers.

three miles up the harbour, it is now used as a store attached to the slaughter-house. On that part of the edifice facing the High-street, in a niche in the wall, is placed a fine bust of the late King Charles I cast in brass and on a stone beneath are the following lines:

" After his Travels through all France and Spain, and having passed very many dangers both by sea and land, he arrived here the the 5th day of October, 1623."

A little lower down the High-street stand the Point Gates, built, or perhaps more probably repaired, by King James II, as appears from an inscription still legible over the principal archway. This part of the town is completely insulated at high water and communicates with Portsmouth by means of a drawbridge. Near the bottom of Broad-street, on the right hand, is situated the Custom-house, a spacious edifice, well calculated for the mercantile business of this Port and its neighbourhood. The present establishment consists of one Collector, one Comptroller, eight Clerks, two Surveyors, four Landing-waiters, one Searcher, three Coast-waiters, two Tide Surveyors, two Warehouse-keepers, six Lockers, fifty Tide-waiters, besides a large number of extra men occasionally employed.

Portsmouth was formerly a member port, belonging to the mother port of Southampton, but this is done away with and it does not now depend in the least on it. The extent of this Port is reckoned from *Hell Head* in this county to the west end of the *Brambles*, a shoal between this place and the Isle of Wight, and from thence in a direct line to the point of land in that island, called Bembridge Point, and then N. E. to the most easterly point of Hayling Island: thence up the stream to Emsworth and back again, near Southsea Castle, in this harbour, and then up the stream to Fareham, and back again to the *Town Key* of Portsmouth.

In the year 1798, the Imports at this Custom-house were £79,000;

Coast Duties, £15,500; Exports, £2,000. The duties on wine only were in the same year £22,000, which was increased in the year 1815 to the large amount of £137,912!

The important *Quarantine* Establishment, stationed at the Motherbank, is a branch of this office, which has two tenders employed under it. The present Custom-house was erected in the year 1785. The place where the merchant ships lie is a part of the harbour lying between the Gun wharf and the Point, contiguous to the Town Quay, which communicates with Portsmouth by a large and grand gate, called *Quay Gate*, leading directly to the Victualling Office, and with Portsea, by means of a road which passes the King's Mill and the Gun wharf.

In the year 1754, was built by subscription a commodious Bathing-house, situated near the mouth of the harbour, close to the run of the tide, which plentifully supplies four baths of different depths of water; two of them are large enough to swim in. In this Bathing-house are likewise hot baths and two good dressing-rooms: one for ladies, the other for gentlemen; and every other necessary accommodation.

For those who are fearful of bathing in the open sea this must undoubtedly be a great advantage, and it is a matter of astonishment that Southampton (whose waters are of a mixed kind, partly fresh and partly salt) should be preferred to Portsmouth for the purpose of bathing; for certainly the large flux and reflux of *pure* salt water at this place must render it infinitely superior in many cases where sea water is recommended as necessary.

At the lower end of *St. Thomas's-street* stands the *Church*, a venerable pile, dedicated to the celebrated but martyred *Thomas à Becket, Archbishop of Canterbury*. There are no accounts remaining by which the precise period of its erection can be ascertained, but it was certainly built by *Peter de Rupibus*, Bishop of Winchester, between the years 1210 and 1220, for in the agreement between the *Prior of Southwick* and the *Master* and *Brothers* of *Domus Dei* (cited above) it is there called the NEW Mother Church, from which we must readily infer that no very considerable number of years had elapsed since the foundation of the edifice.

About the year 1230, *Thomas Eynolf*, an inhabitant of *Portsmue*, dying, bequeathed several legacies to many of the Priests belonging to the Church, and also a sum of money to be received yearly towards its reparations.

In the year 1260 a deed was executed between the *prior* and *convent* of *Southwick* and *Thomas de Sengelton*, vicar of this church, by which the said vicar was to enjoy and receive all the *titles* and *oblations* of the *Town of Portesmuth* on paying to the said prior the sum of 100 shillings yearly, &c.

The church of St. Thomas at present consists of architecture of two different periods; the chancel however is by far the most ancient, being almost in the same condition as when first founded by *Peter de Rupibus*. The body of the church has undergone a complete change. The old body and nave were pulled down in the year 1690; the *low tower* which had stood at the intersection of the roof, disappeared, and in the following year the present elegant fabric arose under the auspices of Ambrose Stanyford, Esq, who lies interred in one of the side aisles, and whose tomb here following, commemorates the occasion:—

Beneath this Stone Lyes the
earthly Remaines of Ambrose
Stanyford, who by the good pro-
uidence of God was ye happy instrument of Contriueing Frameing
& finishing ye inside beauty of this
house for ye Glory of God & to ye
Joy & Comfort of his People as-
sembling hear to his Worship.
He departed this Life
the 8th of October, 1694.

At this period there was no tower erected on the church, but a
small buttress on the South side was used as a belfry, which is now
occupied as a bone-house. Nine years after the erection of the nave at
a vestry of the inhabitants in the year 1702, they came to a resolution
of raising a Cupulo on the tower of the Church, which was
accordingly done and William Brandon Esq, mayor in the year 1703,
presented the parish with a musical ring of eight bells, five of which
were given by Prince George of Denmark, who at the request of Sir
George Rook, had them removed from an old Pharos within the
Fortifications of Dover Castle.

In the year 1718, the Church was embellished with a good and well
toned organ, built by Subscription, and erected at the West end of it.
On the left hand side at the grand entrance is the Font, an octangular
stone, carved with quatre-foils, and coats of arms, of great antiquity
and co-eval with the chancel. A porch was built on the outside of the
chancel door in the year 1731, for the greater warmth and
convenience of the congregation. In the year 1750 the cupulo and
lanthorn were repaired; and a seat likewise erected in the North

gallery for the use of the charity children; and in the year 1768, the church-yard was embellished with new piers and cast-iron gates.

At the back of the communion table in the chancel is an handsome monument, erected in the year 1631 to the memory of the Duke of Buckingham (who had been assassinated in this town in the reign of Charles I) by his sister, Susannah, Countess of Denbigh: which bears the following inscription:---

GEORGIO VILLERIO BVCKINGHAM: DVCI
Qvi Maioribvs vtrinq Clarissimis
Orivndvs; patre *Georgio Villerio De*
Brooksby in Comit: Leicestr: Milit:
Matre Maria Beamovnt Bvckingh.
Comitissæ Cvnctis natvræ fortvnæq
Dotibvs insignis Dvorv Prvden
tissimorv Principvm gratia
Svisq mentis,vota svorvm
Svpergress Rervm Gerendarv,
Moli Par soli iuvidiæ impar
Dvm Exercitvs iterv in hoste
Parat hoc in Opido Cædis
Imaniss: Fatali arena novo
Crvoris et Lachrimar invad-
ante Oceano nefaria perditissimi
Sicarii manv.

Percussvs Occvbvit
Ano Dni MDCXXVIII: Mense Avg; Die xxiii.
Viro ad omnia quæ maxima
essent nato Eiusq et svis Hic

vna Confossis visceribvs.
Svsanna Soror Denbighiæ Comitissa
Cvm Lachrimis et Ivetv perpetvo
P.

Ano Dni: MDCXXXI.
Tv Viator si qva tibi pietatis
Viscera tam indignv Tanti
Viri Casvm indignabvndvs
Geme,

Et Vale.

Translation.

Sacred to the Memory of *George Villiers Duke of Buckingham*,
son of the illustrious *Sir George Villiers* of Brooksby, in the County of
Leicester, and *Mary Beaumont*, Countess of Buckingham, who
possessed in an eminent degree the gifts of nature and fortune,
together with the favour of two most excellent Princes: his exalted
abilities exceeding the expectations of all men, rendered him *equal* to
the weight of the highest employments of state, *unequal* alone to the
shafts of envy. Whilst he was preparing his army to a second attack of
the enemy, he fell on the 23d of August 1628, by the impious hand of
an accursed assassin, the fatal shore being inundated with an ocean
of blood and tears. In commemoration of his many excellencies, and
the loss she has sustained in him, his inconsolable Sister, *Susanna,
Countess of Denbigh,* erected this monument in the year 1631.

Reader if thou hast any yearnings of affection within thee, bewail
with indignation the undeserved fall of this great man. Farewell.

In a Register book belonging to this church[85] is preserved the marriage entry of King Charles the II and Catherine, Infanta of Portugal, finely illuminated it is as follows:—

Our Most Gracious Soveraigne Lord Charles the Second by the Grace of God King of Great Brittaine France and Ireland Defender of the Faith &c. And the most Illustrious Princesse Dona Catarine Infanta of Portugall (daughter to the deceased) DON JUAN the

---

85 In the years 1615 and 1633, the following benefactions occur to the church:—

"Item, Sir John Burlace, Governour of Portsmouth dide gyve at ye Baptm of his childe fower hangines to ye churche, one for ye pulpitt, one for the comunion tabell, one for ye gouernores seate, and one for ye mayer: too of them clothe of gold, and one of them imbroidered on both sides, and one of them redd veluett theye weare opened thys 24th of Avgust 1615.

"Item, John Trigger, church-wardene, and Roger Pricey, dide caste ye 4th bell anno domini 1632: and a newe bibell which cost thirti shillinges, and a newe tabel Cloth for the Comvnion which coste thirteene shillinges 1633."

The following inventory of this Church, taken A. D. 1636, will enable the reader to form a correct idea of its importance at that period :—

"One newe bible, twoe Bookes of Comon prayer, Bishoppe Jewell's workes, one siluer Chalice with a couer to him, twoe pewter Flaggons for the Comunion Table, twoe surplices, twoe diap table clothes, and twoe napkins of diap, one table cloth of branched damaske beeing red and yallow, one cushion and cloth belonging to the pulpitt of the same damaske; one Pall the bed of it cloth of gold.

"Twoe faire Cushions of cloth of gold, laced with gold lace, one nedle worke cushion for the pulpitt wrought on both sides with gold silke & siluer, one cushion for the comunion table of red veluet, imbroadered wth gold.

"These 4 cushions were giuen by that Worthy Knt. Sir John Burlace to remaine successiuely in the said pishe Church for ever, to the vse of the saide pishe Church, and noe otherwise.

FOURTH and Sister to the Present DON ALPHONSO, Kings of Portugall) were married at Portsmouth uppon thursday the two & twentieth day of May in the year of our LORD GOD 1662 being in the fourteenth year of his Maties reigne by the Right Reuerend Father in God Gilbert Lord Bishop of London Dean of his Maties Chappel Royall, in the presence of Seuerall of the Nobility of his Maties Dominions & of Portugall.   *ANNO DNI 1662*

"Fower bells, in the Tower,

" One Saint's Bell on the topp of the Church,

" Twoe small Bells for the Quarter Clocke,

"One Great Clocke,

"One Quarter Clocke, and

"One paire of Chimes."

"November the 12th, 1687.

"This day a certaine parcel of plate (the particular pieces whereof are underneath mentioned) was presented to the Mayor, Aldermen, and Burgesses of the borough of Portesmouth, in their Town-hall assembled, which plate was freely given by his Gracious Majesty, our present Soveraigne Lord King James the Second, for the use of the parish Church of Portesmouth; and is as followeth :

"Imprimis,   Two faire siluer Flagons, plaine,

"Item,   One faire siluer Chalice,

"Item,   Two faire large siluer patters,

"Item,   One small siluer patter.

"The whole parcell weighing one hundred and nineteene ounces.

" J. Grundy, Mayor,   Tho. Heather, Vicar,

" Isaac Betts,   John Taylor, Churchwarden

" Thos. Hancocke, John Blose."

We here subjoin an account of the Communion Plate and other Church goods, as taken in the year 1711 :—

On the right hand side of the altar is an ancient monument erected to the memory of Sir Charles Blunt, who died on the sea, whilst returning from Ireland to this kingdom; it bears the following Inscription:

Here vnder resteth ye body of Sir Charles Blovnt, one of her Ma.ts Band of Pencioners 3 sonn of Sr. Mitchall Blovnt, Kt. lineally descended from Walter, first Lord Movntioy. He was from his youth trayned vp in Marshall Affaires: He went over with ye Earle of Leaster in to ye Lowe Cvntries abovght ye age of 15 yeares, wheare

		Ounces.	Dwts.
Flaggons two	One weighing	36	13
	The other	36	0
Chalices two	one weighing	13	15
	the other	12	17
Salvers two	one weighing	13	11
	the other	13	10
Patters two	one weighing	5	5
	the other	5	5
Two large silver Plates for receiving the offering money at the Communion		31	1

One large Crimson Velvet Communion Table Cloth, with gold fringe; and two embroidered Cushions, covered with similar velvet, given by Thomas Ridge, Esq.

One Crimson Velvet Pulpit Cloth and Cushion, and Cloth for the Reading Desk, with gold Fringe and Tassils, given by Nicholas Hedger, Esq.

One large branch of Brass Candlesticks in the Church, a gift from the Hon. Sir John Gibson, Knt. Lieut-Governor of Portsmouth.

Two brass branches of Candlesticks hanging in the body of the Church, presented, to the parish by Capt. John Suffield, together with two brass Sconces for the Pulpit and Reading Desk.

with svch good Circvmspection he carried himself, that for his Valovr he was highly Comended, & from thence retvrning he was imployed in ye warres of Brittayne against ye Spaniards vnder ye Condvction of Generall Norissi, where he vere valiavntly behaved himself, & was there taken Prisoner & ransomed by his Father: At ye iovrney to Cales he went with ye Earle of Essex, where for his good service he receaved ye Order of Knighthood: At ye iovrney into ye Ilandes he went likewise with ye said Earle as Coronell, & lastly he went over into Ireland wJth ye said Earle, & was Coronell & Governor of Caiher Castill. Bvt in his Retvrn hom vppon ye seae he depted ys life in his Prime & florishing yeares abovght ye Age of 32: As his Lyfe was pleasing to his Frendes so his Death yealded comfort to those yt weare present, with assvred Hope of his ioyfull Resvrection he yealded vp his sovle to God, yt first gave it, & his Bodie to ye earth whereof it was made.

On the left hand side of the Altar lies interred the body of Sir John Kempthorne, Knt., who was Commissioner of his Majesty's Navy here in the reign of Charles II. On the stone are inscribed these lines:

> Here lyeth Interred the Body of Sr. John
> Kempthorne Knight who had ye Honour
> to wear severall Flaggs in severall Com-
> mands in his Majests service and hath
> fought severall Battles at sea for his
> King and Country: and dyed Commissio-
> ner of his Majests Navy at Portsmouth
> the 19th day of October 1679
> being aged 59 yeares.

Heare beneath this Stone doth lye,
As much Valour as could dye,
Who in his Life did Vigour giue
To as much Justice as could liue,
But Death (which ne're could him dismay,)
Vnkindly snatcht him hence away.

On a stone fixed in the pavement near the Altar is the grave of Hugh Salesbury, Esq, one of the Mayors of this town in the reign of Charles II. It has simply these words:

IN MEMORIAM
HVIONIS SALESBVRY
GEN: QVI OBIIT 29°:
IVNII 1677.

A Monument, resting against one of the pillars near the North Porch has inscribed on it the following lines:

Memoriæ sacræ
Thom. Heather A. M. sereniss;
Car. 2di. Majestat: a sacris. et
hujus Ecclæ Vicarii.
Qui cu 33 pene annos,
eximiæ pietatis, incorruptæ
fidei et diligentiæ pastoralis, vi-
vendo, credendo, concionando,
spectabile fuisset exemplar:
Animam Deo reddidit 20 die
Mensis xbris, Ann. Dom. 1696:

Ætat, suæ 75. Dormit in pace
corpus, beatam præstolans
Resurrectionem, sed trIste sub
desiderium amicis reliquit,
Vale Lector et (ut
ex animo *Valeas*)
Vive bene.

Near this, is

In Memoriam
Viri Reverendi
Beniaminis Bvrgess Artvim Magister
Ervditione, Pietate, Prvdentia
Morvm svavitate insignis
Evangelii Præco'nis fidelissimi
Ecclesiæ hie Loci nuper
Pastoris Vigilantissimi,
Qui obiit 24° Novemb. Aimo Dom. 1673
Ætatis suæ 44°

In the Church-yard, without the North Porch is a stone to the
memory of Sarah the wife of Nicholas Belbin, Esq, whose brother was
Mayor of this town during the Protectorate of Oliver Cromwell.

Here lyeth bvried
Sarah the Wife of
Nicholas Belbin
Aged 23 years
Who deceased on
The 1st of Janvary
1680 -

The Chancel of this Church is about 44 feet in width and the Body of the Church near 112 feet in length. The walls round the burial ground were either built or repaired in the year 1645, as appears from the following words carved on a stone, placed in that part of the yard that faces Golden Lion Lane :—

> **STEVEN**
> **WHELLER**
> **1645**

The Tower is 120 feet high, and over the Cupola is a lanthorn with a bell in it, formerly employed to give notice how many ships appeared in the Offing, for which purpose a watchman was kept there, but it is now only employed in case of fire. Above this lanthorn, instead of a weathercock, is a ship completely rigged, about six feet in length from stem to stern, which has a pleasing effect.

At the upper end of St Thomas's-street is the residence of the Lieutenant Governor Lord Howard, an elegant and convenient edifice fitted up in an handsome manner by Government. In this street some short distance lower down, on the other side of the way, is the Post-office.

On the right hand side of this is another street, called formerly *Hogmarket-street*, but now known by the name of *Warblington-street*, towards the upper end of which is situated the Poor-house, a large spacious building erected about the beginning of last century.

The only principal street on the left is Penny-street, in which a very large and handsome Gaol has been erected pursuant to Act of

Parliament, A.D. 1806, where are held four Sessions of the Peace yearly, a Court of Record on Tuesday in every week, in which Court any person may sue for a debt not under forty shillings. At the Sessions are tried all petty larcenies and other small offences, but nothing capital can be determined here. A little below it is an Alms-house, endowed by a Mr. Burgess for eight poor widows; and in addition to the legacy left them by the above gentleman, Mr. Mounsher, by will in 1702 gave the sum of Five Pounds yearly for ever, to the *poor widows* of Portsmouth not receiving alms of this parish.

In this Street is also a Grammar-school under the patronage of the Dean and Chapter of Christ Church, Oxford, founded by Dr. Smith, an eminent physician of this place, in the year 1732. In this school are taught the classics; and the mathematics, writing and arithmetic are carried on under the direction of *Mr. Thomas Martin*, an excellent master.

At the lower end of St. Mary's-street, was, some years since, an ancient building in which was an Armory for 5,000 men. The arms were kept in the greatest order and regularity and disposed of with such taste as to be worthy the observation of all; it is, however, now done away with. Where the Barracks near this street now stand was formerly a religious house called *St. Mary's*, the burying ground of which, called *Colewort* Garden, (probably from the circumstance of its having been used as a *colewort* or *cabbage* garden for the Priory), is still in use; and here we cannot help observing the great alteration for the better that has taken place in the appearance of this garden; from being one of the most *disgraceful* places of interment in the kingdom it has been rendered one of the handsomest, most decent, and improved burial-grounds that can possibly be conceived, and we must add, that the Churchwardens undoubtedly deserve our thanks for the vast exertions they must have taken to bring it from its former state into that we at present have the pleasure of beholding it.

In King's-street stands the Victualling Office, a large building with an handsome edifice for the residence of William Reeks, Esq, the Agent Victualler. Opposite this building is a storehouse, so large as to extend the whole length of the street; in those warehouses, provisions are stored in vast quantities for the use of the navy; pork and beef salted; biscuit baked, and every other article of provision for the service of the navy.

There are four Barracks in this town, two occupied by the regiments on duty, one by the Artillery, and the fourth by the Marines of this division, who are stationed here that they may be in readiness to embark on board the ships as they are wanted; however, since the peace they have assisted in doing the duty of the garrison, and consequently the number of troops here have been considerably reduced. The Barracks, called *Fourhouse Barracks*, situated near the Marine Barracks, are so commodious as to be able to accommodate upwards of 1,000 men, with every convenience for them and their officers.

The population and number of houses in this town and neighbourhood, are thus stated in the returns made under the Act in 1801:—

The number of houses in Portsmouth	1134
Of Inhabitants	7839
The number of houses in Portsea	2554
Of Inhabitants	14943
Houses in the Liberty of Portsea, in that part within the Borough	1651
Inhabitants	9384
Houses in the Guildable part, beyond the	

The town of Portsmouth was anciently defended by a wall of timber covered with earth; Leland has given us this description of the fortifications, in the reign of Henry VIII. *"The towne of Portesmuth is murid from the est tour a forough lengthe with a mudde waulle armid with tymbre, whereon be great peaces both of yren and brassen ordinauns; and this peace of the waulle hauing a diche without it, rennith so far flat south south-est, and is the place most apte to defend the town ther open on the hauen. Ther rennith a diche almost flat est for a space, and wythin it is a waulle of mudde like to the other, and so thens goith rounde about the toun to the circuite of a myle. Ther is a gate of tymbre at the north este ende of the toun, and by it is caste up an hille of erths diched, wherein be gunnes to defend entre into the toun by land."*

Such was the simple way in which this town was anciently fortified, and to the weakness of which it owes all the disasters it formerly underwent in the years 1265 and 1377, in both of which years it was burnt and levelled to the ground: however, in the reign of King Edward VI great improvements were made in the fortifications which had been began in the reign of Edward IV. Charles II, after his restoration, made great alterations, raised several forts and fortified them after the modern manner, which works were augmented in the reign of James II, since which time this place has received great additions from succeeding Princes, so that at present it is the most regular fortress in Great Britain, and as it cannot be effectually attacked by sea, may very justly be deemed impregnable.

The town is nearly surrounded by the ramparts, which are about a mile and a quarter in circumference, edged with elm trees, whose spreading foliage affords one of the most delightful promenades that can possibly be conceived. From this eminence the beautiful view of the sea, contrasted with the landscape which the surrounding country affords, form one of the most striking and variegated scenes imaginable. Indeed it has been an object of the highest admiration to strangers, and we may venture to affirm, will ever continue so, as long as the beauties of nature and art continue to merit our attention.

We shall now conclude our account of the present state of this town with a concise description of the harbour of Portsmouth:

This harbour is the principal one in the kingdom and the most distinguished part of is *Spithead*, situated between the continent of Hampshire and the Isle of Wight; it is about twenty miles in length and in some places three miles in breadth. It is capable of receiving the whole navy of England, and the depth of water is so great that the first-rate man of war can ride at the lowest ebb without touching ground. Spithead takes its name from a sand bank, which extends from the right side of the harbour running towards Southsea Castle and ending in a point, which is called the *head* of the *Spit* or *Spithead*.

It is hoped the reader will not judge the following description of this noble *road* from a recent author[86] unnecessary, as it will plainly show the great importance which is attached to Spithead, as an anchorage and place of *rendezvous* for our navy.

"The Haven of Portsmouth is so well known, as to require no particular description; yet to demonstrate its superiority to other Ports, we will examine the characteristics of a perfect harbour, laid down by the ablest writers on Naval affairs, premising that they give these only as ideal marks of what according to their conception should belong to a place deserving that title; and that the

---

86 Campbell

comparative value of these that really exist, may be the better understood.

"The *first* then is, that it be so situated, and of such a figure, as to be secure from all dangers, as least from most winds:— The harbour of Portsmouth is so covered by the towns of Portsmouth and Gosport, the Common, the Blockhouse, Gunwharf, Dock-yard, Plantations, and the high hill of Portsdown, that the wind cannot blow from any point of the compass to the detriment of the ships at anchor therein.

"The *second* rule is, that it be of a proper depth so that ships of any size may lie securely without raking their bottom:— This port is so deep that a first-rate at the lowest ebb can ride, without touching the ground, and as she lies at anchor, can take in her sea stores and guns and be out of the harbour in half an hour.

"The *third* is, that the bottom be sound and fit for anchoring:— In respect to this no harbour more exactly answers the description than that of Portsmouth.

"The *next* requires, that there be no hidden rock, shelves, sands, or other trouble-some impediments:— from all these this haven is entirely exempt.

"The *fifth* demands that it should be capacious, so as to hold a large number of ships with ease and safety, and if possible divided into several branches:— this noble port is so capacious that it can conveniently contain the whole Royal Navy, or at least as great a part thereof as is ever laid up in ordinary.

"The *sixth* requisite is, that there be no bars or other obstructions to embarrass the entrance, and which may render the access difficult or dangerous :— Portsmouth harbour is not broader at the mouth than the Thames at Westminster, and as the water flows *seven*, and ebbs but *five* hours, the flux is greater out than in; so that the bottom is always scowering, and the water running out at an angle throws the bar to the S.W. which is called the *Spit*, and leaves a deep channel close under the shore to South-sea Castle.

"The *next* demands, that the sides or the mouth be well protected by forts, blockhouses and other fortifications, more especially if it be seated immediately upon the sea:— there is scarce any thing in this respect wanting that could be wished at Portsmouth.

"The *eighth* position is, that there be an arsenal for building and repairing ships commodious in all respects, and more especially for launching them:— The yard of Portsmouth is so convenient that it has not its equal; here are five docks one of them so large as to admit *two* ships at a time, so that *five* may be docked and cleaned in a *day*, while the spring tides continue, that is between *forty* and *fifty* in a month; and the improvements made here for setting masts and rigging with the utmost dispatch are such as would demand a long description.

"The *next* is, that there be plenty of naval stores ammunition and provision of every sort: — It may be affirmed there is no place in Europe where these are to be found better in their respective kinds, in larger quantities, or in more complete order.

"The *last* is, that there be a constant and sufficient garrison for the security of the port against any sudden attempt to surprise, or any descent that may be made to reduce it. — This there is at Portsmouth, which is now a town regularly fortified in the modern stile; and the *Common*[87] Dock-yard and Gun-wharf are likewise so effectually secured that it would necessarily require a very numerous army to invest and besiege it; nor could it then be taken without affording time sufficient for its relief.

"A further and indeed very capital convenience to the harbour of

---

87 Now Portsea.

Portsmouth is the safe and spacious road of *Spithead*, which lies
between the continent of Hampshire and the Isle of Wight; and is
about twenty miles in length, and in some places no less than three in
breadth; so that it is capable of holding a *thousand* ships at a *time*,
without the least difficulty or danger: it is defended from all winds
blowing from the W. to the S. E. by the high lands of the *Isle of
Wight*; and from the winds of the opposite quarter by the mainland
of *Hampshire*. The town of Portsmouth fronting the middle of the
road, the very sands in its neighbourhood contribute to its safety; as
for instance, the *spit* lying to the N breaks the sea on that side, as the
horse's bank, does to the E, and *No mans land* and the *Motherbank*
on the S. As to the bottom, it is perfectly sound and good, and the
flux and *reflux* of the sea repairs all the injuries done by the
anchors[88]."

---

88 *Gilpin* in his *Tour* through *Hampshire* thus describes the *Road* of
Spithead:— "Before the mouth of Portsmouth harbour runs out (like a vast
court before the front gate of a castle) the noble road of *Spithead*. It takes its
name from a *Sandbank*, which extends from the right side of the harbour,
running towards Southsea-Castle, and ending in a point which is called the
head of the *Spit*, or *Spithead*. Round this point, under the batteries of
Southsea-Castle, all ships must pass that go from Portsmouth harbour into
Spithead road, which stretches five or six leagues; and it is well secured from
every wind, by the *folding* of the lsle of Wight over the Hampshire coast.
Here the fleets of England ride in safety, till they are fully reinforced by the
several ships intended to join them, as each is equipped, and leaves the
harbour."

CHAPTER IV

Of Portsea, the Gun-wharf, Dock-yard, &c.

FROM the great and progressive increase of the naval establishments and trade of Portsmouth, and the vast augmentation of houses within its walls, this town was rendered by far too small for its population; accordingly early in the last century, an open common situated on the north side, was selected as the most convenient place for erecting additional edifices. As these in time became inhabited, new ones were built, and were again rapidly increased by others, till the new buildings assumed the appearance of a spacious suburb, called for many years by the name of *Portsmouth Common*. Still increasing with astonishing rapidity, the *offspring* out-grew its *parent* town, which lying within the old fortifications, presented no vacant ground for erections. Assuming consequence with extent, its original title of the *Common* was laid aside and in an act of Parliament passed in the year 1792 for paving and improving the place, it displayed its rising honours under the appellation of the *Town of Portsea*.[89]

---

89 The *Island of Portsea* is, as we have already stated, about sixteen miles in circumference, and the ride round it affords one of the most delightful excursions that can possibly be conceived. During the *Heptarchy* it was a *Royal Demesne*, but alienated in the reign of *Edgar*, by *Athelfleda*, his Queen bestowing it as an addition to the *new minster* at *Winchester*, which still retains a large portion of it as *collegiate land*. It consists of *two* parishes, viz. that of *Portsmouth and Portsea*, the *extra parochial* land of the *Salterns* and *Hilsea*, but this latter forming a part of the parish of Wymering, is not to be considered further than including it in the aggregate number of acres, amounting to about 4350, of which about 3200 are arable, 400 pasture, 620

About a quarter of a mile distant from the *quay* gates in the road to the dock-yard is situated the king's mill, a large building of brick raised on piles, twenty-five or thirty feet long, shod with iron, driven into a marshy ground. The mill is worked by a stream of salt water coming from the harbour at every tide, which is received by means of a sluice into a large basin close to the mill, and contiguous to a part of the works; the sluice is let down at high water, and when the tide has ebbed for some little time, the water is worked back again into the harbour. Most of the grain used in the Victualling Office in King's street is ground at this mill, as would likewise the corn for the service of the navy and garrison in case of a siege. The expense of this building to Government was between six and £7000.

A little beyond the mill is the *gun-wharf*, the grand arsenal for

common, and 130 acres of waste land belonging to government. There are but few sheep in the Island of Portsea, owing in some measure to the great quantity of land which is devoted to the purposes of supplying hay and grass for cattle, and the production of vegetables; and the small quantity of sheep are commonly purchased at the autumn fairs. Broccoli and cauliflowers here are particularly excellent, and although the seed of these vegetables is frequently sown in other parts, yet it has never been known to produce any in such perfection as in the gardens near Portsmouth. The common fields, according to the *ancient* customs of this borough are to be driven by the chamberlain immediately after harvest is in. The owner of every horse who has no right to the common fields, is to pay for each horse the sum of 6s. 8d. For every cow 3s. 4d. and for every sheep or pig 4d. And for every five acres of land any person has in the common fields, he is entitled to keep one horse, or two cows, or twenty sheep or pigs. Every Burgess belonging to this corporation, has a right to feed one horse in the common fields during the time they remain open; and the corporation were entitled formerly to have from the respective owners, the sum of three pence an acre for every acre of land in the common fields, which has been many years since done away with.

cannon, mortars, bombs, carcases, carriages and ball of all dimensions. It has been impossible to ascertain when it was first established, but it is supposed to have been so, nearly about the time the dock-yard was formed, as the two departments are closely connected together. Ships are supplied from this arsenal with guns, shot, and every kind of ordnance stores, except gun-powder which is obtained from the magazine at Pridday's Hard, near Gosport. There is an armory here for small arms, which are arranged in excellent order, and several large storehouses fitted with every kind of stores for the sea and land service; likewise there are two smiths' shops, two carpenters' shops a collar-maker's shop and one for armourers. Every ship in ordinary has on the wharf her guns, placed in regular rows, each ship's guns by themselves, with the name of the ship they belong to painted in capital letters on the first gun of each parcel. The balls are formed in pyramids from 42 pounders to the lowest bores, every size in a pyramid by themselves; the bomb shells are also placed in the same regular order. There are many handsome and genteel houses, exclusive of the offices, for the officers of the yard to reside in, and in the front of these buildings are planted rows of trees which have a very pleasing effect. The present establishment consists of three officers, *viz* a storekeeper, a clerk of the survey, and clerk of the cheque; also six established clerks (to which are added in time of war three assistants), eight foremen, eighty artificers, about sixty labourers, three porters and two office messengers; at the entrance to the gunwharf is a lodge for the master porter. Many expeditions for foreign service to a very considerable extent are fitted out at this wharf, and embarked with the greatest facility and despatch.

At a short distance from the Gun-wharf is situated the *Dock-yard*, which is undoubtedly the largest naval arsenal in the world. It has the appearance of a town, from the number of its dwelling-houses, storehouses, offices, and other edifices erected for the purpose of carrying on the various employments of the yard. During the last war there were no less than 5000 workmen employed in it, and at present the establishment consists of between three and four thousand men.

The Commissioner's house, near the entrance of the yard, is a very elegant and spacious edifice surrounded by trees. The present Commissioner is the Hon Sir George Grey, Bart. There is a row of well built brick houses in a part of the yard, for the builder, the clerk of the cheque, store-keeper, clerk of the survey, the master's attendants, &c. In front of this row is a beautiful double gilt statue of King William III, standing on a marble pedestal, the gift of Colonel Richard Norton of Southwick. On it is inscribed:

GVLIELMO

III.

OPTIMO REGI

MDCCXVIII.

Ricardus Norton humillime D. D.

There are at present in the yard eight Docks, *viz* Camber Head, Camber Stern, North Dock, North Dock in the Basin, Middle Dock, South Dock in the Basin, South East Dock in the Basin, and South Dock; the five last of these are capable of holding first-rates; there are likewise two for third-rates, and five building slips. The following ships are at present building in the yard:--

The Princess Charlotte	Minerva
Talavera	Samoray
Carnatic Minerva	And the Prince
	Regent yacht.

The Rope House, in which cables are made, is 1094 feet long by 54 broad; the spinning-house over it is of the same dimensions; some of the cables are so large as to require eighty men to work them, who from the laboriousness of the business are unable to continue at it above four hours in the day.

A Royal Naval College is established here; the first Lord of the Admiralty is Governor of it, and the Lieutenant-Governor is a Post Captain, who resides in apartments attached to the College. There is also appointed to it a Professor of Mathematics, a Preceptor and two Assistants, with French, Drawing, Fencing, and Dancing Masters for the tuition of the students; in addition to the above, a Matron superintends the domestic concerns of the Establishment and two Serjeants of the Royal Marine Artillery instruct them in the use of cannon. A School of Naval Architecture has been recently established, for the instruction of youth in the art of shipbuilding, from which the officers in that line are in future to be selected.

In one of the rooms belonging to the College is a superb model of the Victory, a first-rate ship of war, built in this yard, and unfortunately lost with the brave Admiral Bulchen near the Race of Alderney in the year, 1744. This ship mounted 110 brass cannon and had on board 1000 men, all of whom perished. The model is about five feet long from the tafferel to the head, and was built in this yard at an amazing expense; all the running rigging is twisted silk, the carved work on the head and stern is very minute and beautiful; it is preserved in a glass case, and is really, without exaggeration, a most valuable piece of workmanship. Under a glass cupola in the same room, is a very fine Orrery constructed by the ingenious artist, Mr. Wright. Near the academy is an Observatory, furnished with every necessary instrument proper for the uses for which it was raised.

A short distance from hence stands the Chapel for divine service. The Blacksmith's Shop, where all the anchors and iron-work are wrought for the service of the navy, is the next structure that claims our attention. Some of the anchors weigh from forty to eighty hundred weight.

This shop strikes the spectator at first view with the remembrance of the fabulous story of the forge of Vulcan, and the workmen bring to his recollection the figures of the Cyclops. The immense masses of the anchors, the ponderous hammers, the vast size of the bellows[90], the roaring of the flaming furnaces, the reverberations of the falling hammers and the fiery pieces of metal flying in all directions, are truly grand and awful.

Within these few years, Steam Engines have been introduced into the yard for the purpose of manufacturing blocks, rolling of copper sheets, bolts, &c, necessary for carrying on the repair of, and building of, men of war.

---

90 These bellows are so large as to require a windlass, and a man, who is partly suspended by slings under his arms, aids the working of them by standing upon two, and pressing one down with his foot alternately as the other rises.

This yard, according to an account left in a manuscript by Thomas Waite, Quarterman, who came into the yard in the year 1650, had at that time no mast-house, no dry-dock, not above 100 shipwrights, and only one team of horses. Another account is likewise given by Isaac Hancock, Quarterman, who came into the yard A. D. 1661. He has left a memorandum of his having heard that his grandfather, John Hatch, was builder in this yard in the reign of Queen Elizabeth. At that time there was no dry dock, nor afterwards, until the taking of Jamaica. He was then a servant.

At this period there were only-one hundred shipwrights, and about forty or fifty labourers. The Commissioner's house was begun in the year 1664, and completed in 1666. From these MSS may be seen the amazing energy that has been exerted to raise in less than a century and a half, the Dockyard from such a low state of insignificance to its present national importance.

The following is a list of the Surveyors of the Navy in this Dock-yard from the reign of Charles II to the present time :—

Sir William Battin, July, 1660.	Sir Thomas Slade
Thomas Middleton, Esq.	William Bateley, Esq.
Sir John Tippets	John Williams, Esq.
Edmund Dummer, Esq.	Edward Hunt, Esq.
Daniel Fuzer, Esq.	Sir John Henslow
William Lee, Esq.	Sir William Rule
Sir Jacob Ackworth	Joseph Tucker, Esq.
Sir Joseph Allen	Sir Henry Peake
	Robert Seppings, Esq.

A more minute description of this yard would engross more room than our plan will permit; suffice it to say that it furnishes every article for the completion of our ships. And whilst the attention of the reader is upon his subject, we will proceed to give some account of two dreadful fires which happened in the yard some years ago.

On the 3rd of July, 1760, just after midnight, a dreadful fire broke out in the Dock-yard, in one of the principal warehouses, wherein was deposited pitch, tar, oil and turpentine, with vast quantities of other combustible materials, which it soon reduced to ashes; but it did not stop here, for having communicated itself to another warehouse in which were prodigious quantities of dry stores, it raged with an amazing and dreadful rapidity. According to the most general opinion it was set on fire by lightning, and indeed not without great reason was it supposed to be so; for a night of severer thunder and lightning was scarcely ever remembered; and as all, or most of the windows of the lofts where the hemp was deposited were left open to air it, the season being uncommonly sultry, its taking fire was not to be wondered at, from the intense heat of the atmosphere. As the lightning was accompanied with a very heavy rain the chief part of the night, happily the conflagration did not extend through the whole yard. The loss on this occasion was immense, but such was the very great assiduity of Administration in making good the damage it had sustained that the whole was in a few months put into as perfect a state as prior to the occurrence of this accident.

This accident, lamentable as it was in its nature, was only the forerunner of one which happened ten years after, in so tremendous a manner as almost to threaten the utter extinction of our naval power at this port. The particulars of it are as follow :

On the 27th of July, 1770, about three o'clock in the morning, it is generally supposed to have commenced, for it is not well known who first discovered it, but from some circumstances, it appears to have been the centinels on duty, as about five o'clock in the morning, a gentleman in his study saw a prodigious smoke proceeding from the rope-house, which alarmed him much, and he was going to acquaint the officers on duty of it, when he heard the drums beat to arms and very soon after saw the whole Dock-yard as it were in flames.

The house where the pitch and tar were lodged was in a short time reduced to ashes. And soon after, the fire broke out in four other different places and burnt with such violence that it threatened the destruction of the whole yard; the inhabitants were filled with the utmost consternation, but by the shifting of the wind, together with the assistance of the artificers, the seamen and marines, the progress of the flames was stopped about three in the afternoon.

The time of the fire breaking out and the confusion which seized all ranks of people prevented such timely enquiries being made as to afford authentic particulars of the rise of this dreadful event. The accounts mostly to be depended on are that the fire was seen first to burst from the laying-house, about the middle, from whence the flames soon communicated to the spinning-house, owing to some temporary sheds erected between the two buildings, from whence they reached to the oar-house, and set fire to the carpenter's shop, at which time the other store-houses caught, the flames spreading as far as the mast-house, so that in a few hours, masts, cables, and the most valuable materials of the yard, were totally consumed. The carpenter's shop and mast-house were entirely destroyed. The total loss was estimated at an immense sum. By the unwearied exertions, however, of government, the above losses (which in themselves would have been sufficient to have ruined some states!) were repaired in about the short space of *eighteen months*.

Portsea has been paved by Act of Parliament like Portsmouth, and the government and regulation of it, as well as that of every other municipal department, is vested in the Corporation of this town. There are many streets in Portsea. The names of the principal are Queen-street, St. James's-street, Union, Bishop, Hanover, College, Daniel, Cross, North, Prince George's, King, and Cumberland streets. The most respectable part of Portsea is supposed to be St. George's-square, situated near the Gun wharf, in the centre of which was erected some years ago, pursuant to Act of Parliament, a handsome Chapel; the inside is extremely neat, the roof being supported by four well proportioned pillars. This Chapel was built by subscription, the corporation of Portsmouth accommodating the parishioners with the ground on which it is erected.

In the Old Rope Walk is a charitable Institution, held at the Society-hall there, in which a number of indigent children are educated and instructed in the principles of religion and morality. The lower part of the edifice is used as the school-room, and the upper part, being very spacious, is often appropriated for concerts and balls, &c. In addition to the parish workhouses, there are other charitable and humane Societies dependent on St John's Chapel, which the confined limits of our work will not permit us to enumerate. There is a Chapel for Roman Catholics in Prince George's-street, a Synagogue for the Jews in White's row, and many Meeting-houses and Chapels for Dissenters, Baptist, and Methodists.

In the year 1789, a very handsome Chapel was erected in Prince George's-street, and consecrated and dedicated to St. John by the Bishop of Winchester. It has a very elegant appearance on the outside and its inside cannot be viewed by any without the most lively expressions of admiration. The Communion Table is situated in a semi-circular recess, separated by an elegant screen of fluted pillars from the body of the Chapel; it is of marble and the cornice and pannels formed of *stucco*. The arched ceiling is greatly admired for its highly finished *stucco* work, which is exceedingly decorative and appropriate.

There are two very handsome gates in Portsea, called the Lion and Unicorn Gates, which are much admired for the correctness and boldness of their design.

This town, together with Portsmouth, is very abundantly supplied with water by two Companies of Proprietors; but that of the Portsea Island is in the greatest repute, by reason of the peculiar softness of its water; the other concern is conducted by pipes from Farlington, a distance of some miles from Portsmouth.

A Bill is now passing the House of Commons by which it is intended to form a canal between this place and Chichester; much has been said and written both for and against the undertaking, and it is very difficult to determine whether it will ever come to any thing, it being at present only in its infancy. If the design is entered upon, it will have at least one beneficial effect, *viz* that of employing a number of the poor and labouring classes of society.

CHAPTER V
Of Gosport, Haslar Hospital, &c.

THE town of Gosport was, in the reign of Henry VIII, only a village inhabited by fishermen, and it is owing to its vicinity to the Dock-yard and town of Portsmouth that it has acquired all its trade and population. The town consists of three principal streets intersected by others of less magnitude. It has two fairs in, a year, *viz* in October and May, and three markets weekly, on Tuesday, Thursday and Saturday.

Gosport is paved and contains several excellent Inns; it is well supplied on market days with every kind of provisions and vegetables; and there are a number of wherries constantly stationed on the beach to ply the passage from this place to Portsmouth and the vicinity; and the fares, as now regulated by the commissioners, will be found at the end of the work.

At Weovil, near the town, is a large cooperage and brewery established by Government for the use of the navy; at the end of a canal which runs up close to them is a fine basin for the reception of vessels that take in the beer for the supply of the shipping at this port. Weovil was at first only a large private house which was purchased by Government and enclosed with works; to this establishment are connected in war time a vast number of small sloops, which are always kept in readiness to convey beer, &c on board the respective ships that require it.

No great distance from the brewery are some excellent barracks, capacious enough to hold a numerous regiment; north of this is erected an additional barracks for the engineers.

From Weovil, by crossing over Forton Lake you come to *Priddy's*

Hard, a powder magazine for supplying the shipping. The building is arched and bombproof, and there is a small communication with the harbour to facilitate the conveyance of powder to the ships.

The village of *Forton* is situated at the upper end of this lake, which is used as a place of confinement for prisoners of war. The prison consists of a large pile of wooden buildings, forming three sides of an area, inclosed by a high and strong wooden fence guarded by soldiers.

Not far from Forton is situated the very pleasant village of *Alverstoke*, much admired for the beauty of the surrounding landskip; this parish extends from *Crofton* to *Rowner* on the N, until it is bounded by the sea, and thus occupies the greater part of the Peninsula on which the town of Gosport is situated. According to the returns in 1801, the parish of Alverstoke, including the inhabitants of Gosport, was estimated at 11,295, and the number of houses at 1906. The mother church at Alverstoke, is an ancient and venerable edifice and consists of a body and chancel: the interior of it is neat, and the churchyard, which is exceedingly spacious, being planted with trees, forms rather an interesting appearance.

On the west side of the entrance into the harbour, on a spot of ground formerly called Haslar Farm, stands *Haslar Hospital,* a noble and spacious building for sick and wounded seamen and marines, who were before compelled to be put on board hospital ships, where from their being crowded together, though every possible precautions were used to correct the foul air and other ill effects arising from so confined a situation, many valuable lives were lost.

The hospital is situated on a dry gravelly soil within 400 yards of the water, where the sick can land at any time of the tide, and is surrounded with an airing ground, almost a mile in circumference, which is enclosed with a wall twelve feet high. Near the gate is the guardhouse, where a constant guard is kept to prevent riots or desertion, which is able to accommodate a company of soldiers.

It is a regular magnificent brick building, consisting of a front and two wings, each of which is composed of two distinct ranges of building; the front is 567 feet and each of the wings 553 feet in length. On a pediment in front is a handsome sculpture of Portland stone, designed by a Mr Pearce; in the centre are his Majesty's arms, on the right side Navigation is represented leaning one hand on a ship's rudder, and with the other pouring balm from a cruise on a wounded sailor. The north star is over her head and the mariner's compass under her feet. Towards the angle appears the stern of a ship, and quite in the angle are the zephyrs, a group of shells tied together, and a necklace of pearls. On the left side is represented Commerce sitting upon chests and bales of goods, distributing money, fruit and flowers. Towards the angle is a sailor in distress and a bird bringing him an eel in its beak; quite in the angle are Boreas and a group of shells: the shore on which the figures sit is ornamented with shells.

The hospital is surrounded with a handsome *arcade*, twenty-four feet broad, and with the ground on which it is built includes an area of seven acres. The open side of this area contains the chapel, connected to the wings by a row of small stone columns about three feet high with chains; it is a plain neat building, 72 feet long and 36 broad: the burial ground is a separate inclosure beyond the airing ground.

Over the entrance of the hospital is a large hall where the recovering patients reside. This hall is 100 feet in length and 50 in breadth: the wards are all uniform, sixty feet long, and twenty-four broad and have each apartments adjoining for the nurses, with a room for water, which is conveyed from a large reservoir to every part of the building, and from thence below to drains, which are washed by the tide twice in every twenty four hours. Each ward contains ninety patients and the whole hospital is capable of receiving 2,000 men, exclusive of the nurses and necessary attendants.

This building was began in the year 1747 and finished in 1762.

About three quarters of a mile SW of Haslar Hospital is a modern fortification, very strong, and defended with thirty two pieces of ordnance, called *Fort Monkton*; towards the W is a strong redoubt, and this, together with the fort, completely secures this part of the coast. Along the shore to the E, a high and massive stone wall has been erected to preserve the land from the encroachment of the sea.

Near *Fort Monkton* is the *Mother Bank*, well known for being the *rendezvous* of the Indiamen and ships under quarantine. Also near this spot is the buoy which points out the place where the lamentable accident of the Royal George occurred. On the right of this is *Stokes Bay*, a place where merchant and other private vessels generally assemble.

In the harbour and near *Forton Lake* are the ruins of an *ancient castle* or fortification, called *Borough* or *Barrow Castle, traditionally* ascribed to *King Stephen.*

CHAPTER VI
Of Porchester Castle[91].

THE narrow channel or branch of the sea which separates the Island of Portsea from the main land, on the NW side of Langstone Harbour, connects the latter with the *Harbour* of *Portsmouth*, which was a principal *station* of the *Roman Navy*, at the head of which is the strong fortress called *Porchester Castle*. The precise origin of this structure is unknown; but this spot was certainly occupied by a fortress that was successively possessed by the Britons, the Romans, the Saxons, and the Normans; and the various stiles of building practised by the three latter are yet discernible in the towers and

---

91 *Stow* says, that *Porchester Castle* takes its name from the village on which it stands, which was once a town of importance, called *Caer Peris*, built by *Gurgonstus*, the son of *Beline*, who lived 375 years *before* Christ. Another old author says, that it was called by the Britons *Caer Peris,* and was built about the time the City of Rome was founded by *Pereis* or *Perrox* the second son of *Sisil* the founder of *Silchester*, who named it after his own name, and made it the seat of his kingdom. He likewise adds, that this *Sisil* had two sons *Ferrex* and *Perrex*, who in the old age of their father, contended who should succeed him; *Perrox* [sic] attempted by treachery the life of his brother, drove him into Gaul, and at his return though he was aided with the force of that country, defeated and slew him; and then built that Fort or Castle upon the shore, and called it *Caer Peris,* or the *Castle of Perrox* or *Peris*. It is also said to have been the spot where the Emperor Vespasian landed; and was supposed to have had then a famous harbour, but the sea retiring, the inhabitants left the place, and proceeding down to the *mouth* of the *harbour* or port, built a *town* and called it Portsmouth, which is not at all improbable.

walls of the present castle. By the *Britons* it was called *Caer Peris*: this name was altered by the *Romans* to *Portus magnus*, from the Roman name of the harbour; and its modern name *Porchester* is evidently *Saxon*.

The castle is situated on a neck of land, jutting out a considerable way towards the middle of the harbour. It is a noble pile of a *quadrangular* form, surrounding an area of between four or five acres; and still in sufficient preservation to be used as a place of confinement for prisoners of war; from 3000 to 5000 of whom have been secured here at one time.

The walls are from eight to twelve feet in thickness and about eighteen high, having in many places a passage round them covered with a parapet. It has eighteen towers of various shapes and dimensions, including those of the keep; on the NW and S sides are two ditches, varying in breadth, and fifteen feet deep; on the east are two ditches, which extend to the water, and have probably been filled by the influx of the tide. The entrance on the west side is thirty feet deep and fourteen wide under a square tower; on the inside, over the gate, are two projecting figures somewhat resembling Egyptian sphynxes. In the east wall, nearly opposite this gate, is another of similar dimensions: there are likewise two sally ports.

The *Keep* encompasses a *parallelogram* of sixty-five feet by one hundred and fifteen; it has four towers, three of them standing on the outside wall; one of these, which is much larger than the others, forms the NW angle of the square; the fourth tower stands at the SE corner of this building. Here are many rooms, several of them very large, and some arched with stone; amongst them is one which appears to have been a *Chapel*, the entrance through a gate on the south side, only eight feet wide. Several of these towers are now in ruins.

In a more minute description it will be found that the remains of *Roman Architecture* are particularly observable in the outward walls and in the round and semi-circular Towers that defend it at equal distances. The round Towers are placed at the NE, and S.W angles; the NW angle is now taken up by the square Towers of the Keep; some of these towers are twenty, and others nineteen, feet in diameter and generally they project about eighteen feet and a half from the wall. In several rows of them are still visible regular rows of *Roman bricks*, dividing the rows of stone work, and particularly in one on the south side, in which are three rows very distinct; in the wall itself on this side they may be traced, and indeed, in many other places; though from the great alterations made in successive ages the regular courses have in many places been broken off and in others wholly obliterated.

A great *circular* arch of stone, about eight feet in width, on the interior side of the east gate or entrance, has very much the appearance of haying been originally *Roman*, and perhaps, even a remaining part of the identical *Prætorian Portal*. Many Roman Coins and Medals have been dug up here at different times. The extent of the outward walls, exclusive of the projecting parts of the round corner tower, is about 620 feet on the N and S sides, and 610 on the E and W.

In the Keep, which joins the north-west angle of the Castle, traces of the Architecture of the *Saxon* and *Norman* periods and even of yet later ages, to the time of Queen Elizabeth, are plainly to be seen.

The great Tower is lofty, and contains two Vaults or Dungeons at the bottom, with the three remaining double apartments above them in so many several stories: its walls are nearly eight feet thick and its external dimensions on the north and south, fifty-seven feet; and on the east and west, fifty-eight feet. All the light it receives is from narrow loop holes, excepting only in the third story, where on two sides, in what appears to have been state apartments, are small windows in the very plainest *Saxon* style: all the windows are on the sides within the area.

Adjacent to this Tower are the remains of a building which appears to have been subsequently formed as an entrance, the original one having been apparently by a flight of steps on the same side. As a protection to this Tower, which in its original state was most probably *Saxon*, the works now connected with it and which surround the inner court were unquestionably erected in the *Norman* times, and, as supposed, between the period of the *Conquest* and the reign of *Edward I*. Many alterations, however, have been made in this part, and particularly about the time of Edward III, and again in the reigns of Henry VI and VII.

In these additional buildings were a great Dining Hall and various apartments for domestic purposes, with rooms over them for lodging the Garrison and servants and also a grand Staircase leading into the great Tower. But the original destination of all the parts in this quarter of the Castle cannot now be ascertained, as they have been frequently altered during the *last* century. The most curious part, however, of this inner or Norman Court is its fortified entrance, which opens from the outer area on the east.

At the extremity on this side was a *noble portal*, with an obtuse pointed arch, and in this was a great strong gate, about eight feet wide; further on at about sixteen feet and a half from this was a *portcullis*; and beyond that a *second* great gate: eighteen feet more inward still, was beyond this a *second portcullis* and about eleven feet and a half further was a *third* great gate: thus far the whole passage of entrance was only eight feet four inches in width. Nearer the Court, the side walls increase in thickness from four feet nine inches to nearly six feet; and here the entrance passage, which is still continued to the extent of forty-three feet more, becomes wider, its whole breadth being eighteen feet and a half. In this part was designed a place for barricadoes, whilst over the whole vaulted passage, the entire length of which is nearly ninety-four feet, were *perforations* and *machicolations*[92], and to these *machicolations* and to the battlements above was a passage from the top of the surrounding inner court; in this court was a *draw-well*, which still remains open.

The entrance to the outer court or area on the east is by a great *Norman* tower built on the *Roman* works, now much dilapidated, and formerly secured by a *portcullis* and double folding doors, strongly barricadoed. The west or opposite entrance is also by a strong *Norman* tower about thirty-five feet wide and thirty deep; having a passage through the centre about eight feet in width. This also is in ruins.

The *Sacellum* of the Prætorium of the *Romans* is supposed to have been on the spot now occupied as the *scite* of the *Parish Church*, which is an ancient edifice dedicated to St. Mary, standing within the outer court and nearly opposite to the east entrance. Though part of it has been rebuilt and other parts repaired at various times, it still displays *many* specimens of Saxon architecture, particularly in the west front. Its original form was that of a cross with a low tower rising from the intersection; but the south transept has been taken down.

---

92 *Machinolations* were parapets carried from Tower to Tower, on stone brackets, projecting from the wall between them, so has to leave holes, through which the defendants might pour down scalding water, and other annoyances, on those who should attempt to force or fire the portcullis or grate, without being themselves exposed either to danger or view.

All the doors and windows of the ancient part have *semicircular* arches, and those of the west end are decorated with the double *zig-zag* ornaments; the arch of the *west* doorway has likewise some other ornamented mouldings, and all of them spring from *two* columns on each side, with sculptured capitals; the great west window is bricked up.

Here it was that King Henry I founded the *Priory of Black Canons*, afterwards removed to Southwick. Within the Church is a monument erected to the memory of Sir Thomas Cornwallis, Knt Groom Porter to Queen Elizabeth and James I, who died in November 1618. His bust represents him with short hair and beard, and a sash over his shoulders. The font is curious. The Church was returned by the Commissioners at the Dissolution at £30.

In the Rolls of Parliament, the 18th of Edward I, *anno* 1290, a complaint is exhibited against *Henry Huse*, Constable of the King's Castle of *Porchester*, shewing, *"that John, Bishop of Winchester, being absent in foreign parts on the King's service, and all his possessions, being in the King's protection, he, the said Henry, with his armed men, foresters, and others, unknown, hunted at their pleasure in the free chase of the said Bishop."*

In the year 1299, the 27th of Edward I, the Castle and TOWN of *Porchester*, with the forest, then valued at £16 13s, were settled on Queen Margaret as part of her dower.

Among the petitions in the Rolls of Parliament, of uncertain date, there is one to *Edward III*, shewing that on the 15th of Edward II, divers of the *Commonalty of Southampton* were imprisoned in *this* Castle by order of the King, until they had sworn they would make no suit against *Robert Batail* of Winchelsea, the King's Admiral, and *other persons* of the *Cinque Ports*, who had burned and plundered their ships under pretence that the inhabitants were *partizans* of the

Earl of Lancaster, for which outrage they prayed redress. The answer was that every one aggrieved might have a writ of trespass.

It appears from two certificates of discharges for the *Abbot of Glastonbury*, extracted from the register of that house (fol. 128 and 129), that in the 12th of Edward III, *John Hacket,* Lieutenant of the Earl of Arundel, was constable of this Castle; for the defence of which, and the *guard of Portsmouth*, the Abbot was bound to find *three* men at arms for his land in Wiltshire, and *one* for those in Berkshire.[93]

In the 4th year of Edward IV, *anno* 1464, in the Rolls of Parliament, the *Constableship* of this Castle appears to have been granted by *letters* patent of that King, together with the wages and fees thereof, to *John, Earl of Worcester.*

In some grants made in the reigns of Edward V and Richard III, there are the following entries:

"To William Uvedale, Esq, the keeping of the Castle and Tower of Portchester, Portsmouth, and the adjacent country, with the supervision and government of Portsmouth, the places there belonging to the King.

" To William Merfelde, of the keeping of the Castelle of Porchestre, and of the forreste and warren there, and to be supervisore, and governere of the towne of Portysmouth for time of lyfe."[94]

During the reign of Elizabeth, that Princess made several excursions to this Castle.

Porchester Castle descended from the *Norton's* of *Southwick*, in the same manner as their other estates, to the late Robert Thistlewayte, Esq, of whose family it has been rented by government,

---

93 Vide Appendix, No. XVII.

94 Harl. MSS. No. 433.

since it became a place of confinement for prisoners in the late war.

The village of Porchester is about a mile long, ranging on the road to Fareham. The sea rose here so high some years ago in a tremendous storm that boats went up to the very extremity of the village; the banks having, in many places, been broken down by the force of the waves. The publicans of Porchester and Southwick enjoy the peculiar privilege, under charter from Queen Elizabeth, of being exempted from having any soldiers billeted on them or quartered in their houses.

CHAPTER VII

Of the Environs of Portsmouth.

ABOUT three quarters of a mile S of Portsmouth, on the beach of South-sea Common, close to the water's edge, stands Southsea Castle, built by King Henry VIll, in the year 1539,[95] and was *"a ryght goodlie and warlyke castill."* This venerable pile was fortified with a good counterscarp and single moat, with ravelins and single rows of pallisadoes, besides the advanced works, to cover the place from the approaches of the enemy.

Southsea Castle, prior to its present alteration, consisted of work of three different reigns. The interior was a blockhouse, built evidently about the time of Henry VIII, surrounded by a Star Fort of the reign of Charles II, as appeared from the following inscription on a tablet near a flight of steps, which stood on the south-side of the blockhouse:

CAROLVS II. REX.

A. REG. XXXIII.

The whole had been repaired and rendered modern, since the accession of the present Royal Family. This Castle having been for many years in a very decayed and ruinous state, the engineer department have, for the last two or three years, been busily employed in pulling it down and re-erecting it, which is at last

---

95 "This was the time when, in consequence of the alarm of invasion, his majestie in his owne personne toke verie laborious and painfull journeys towardes the sea coastes: and in all doubtfull places caused dyverse and many bulwarkes and fortifications to he made." - HALL'S CHRONICLE.

completed, on the plan of Fort Cumberland, only of far inferior dimensions, to accommodate about 200 men.

King Edward VI, in the year 1552, having been attacked both by the measles and small pox, made a tour through the western and southern parts of England for the recovery of his health, and when he visited Portsmouth, he lay one night in this Castle.

In Peck's *Desiderata Curiosa* is a list of the garrisons belonging to the Crown in the reign of *Queen Elizabeth*, where the following state is given of the garrison of this Castle:

Southsea Castle, Portsmouth	£.	s.	d.
Captaine, fee per diem	0	2	0
Under Captaine, fee per diem	0	1	1
Porters 2, the one per diem	0	0	8
The other	0	0	6
Master gunner, fee per diem	0	0	8
Gunners 14, soldiers 11, one day watch, fee a piece per diem	0	0	6

The taking of this Castle in the year 1642 by the Parliament is thus related in a scarce book,[96] published at the time:

"On Saturday September the third in the night, the parliament forces took *Sousey-Castle* which lyes a mile from the towne upon the sea, and the way thither is on the sea sands. The Captain of the Castle, his name was Challiner, who on Saturday had been at Portsmouth, and in the evening went hope to the Castle and his souldiers took horse-loads of provisions, biscuit, meal and other necessaries with them. They reported he had more drinke in his head

---

96 Jehovah Jireh: God in the Mount, or England's Parliamentarie Chronicle; printed 1644, p. 161.

than was befitting such a time and service, and the townsmen gave
out that he had been bribed with money to yield up the castle, but
t'was false, though the first may be true; yet was not that neither any
furtherance to the taking of it, for thus it was:

"Here were about eighty musqueteers and others that came that
night to the walls of the castle, and under their ordnance, and had
with them a very good engineer, and thirty-five scaling ladders, and
the whole company in the castle, were but twelve officers or
commanders, who all were not able to deal with ours in such a
disadvantage; wherefore ours having suddenly and silently scaled the
walls, called unto them, and advised them what to doe, shewing the
advantage we had over them, and therefore their danger if they
resisted; who seeing the same, immediately yielded the castle to us,
whereupon our triumph at our taking it, was plainly heard about two
of the clock in the morning into the towne; and as soon as they were
masters of the castle, they discharged two pieces of the castle
ordnance against the towne. *The towne of Portesmouth capitulated
the next day.*"

On August the 23d, 1759, about eight o'clock in the morning, part
of this Castle was blown up, by which many lives were lost: the
particulars of this unfortunate accident are as follows:

The regiment, commanded by the Duke of Richmond, being
encamped on Southsea Common, near the Castle, had permission
given them to deposit their powder and ball in the east wing of it. The
day before the accident they had been filling cartridges for the
exercise of the men, of which they had filled nine barrels, with the
ball at the bottom of the barrels; these were placed in a lower room,
over which there was a barrack where two women were washing and
dressing victuals with a large fire of furze.

The flooring of the room being very old, it is supposed that some of the sparks of fire fell through the crevices of the floor on the loose powder the soldiers had carelessly scattered about in their work the day before, and communicated to the barrels, when in an instant, all that quarter of the Castle was blown up with a great explosion, and many people buried under the ruins.

One invalid soldier was blown out of the Castle, above an hundred yards, upon the glacis. He was much blackened by the powder and received a bruise on the head; the centinel, another invalid, was blown over the parapet wall into the dry ditch, one leg and one arm being torn off, which were afterwards found lying on the parapet wall: it is remarkable that one man, as he stood on the wall, some little distance from the fatal spot, escaped without any other hurt than that the instant the explosion happened he was deprived of his senses, and remained for some time in the same position he was in when the event occurred; nor did he stir until being shaken by some people who saw him; he awaked as out of a sleep, without any recollection of what had happened.

There were seventeen men, women and children dug out of the rubbish, all dead except one old soldier, who breathed hard three or four times, and then expired.

The force of the explosion burst open the door of the large magazine to the west quarter of the Castle, where was lodged a great quantity of powder, and tore a large bolt off, but happily it reached no further; all the windows of the Castle were broken, and great part of the whole building damaged; the grand batteries towards the sea were not in the least affected, nor were any of those round the Castle, except in one place a little of the parapet wall towards the land was removed and the top of the wall thrown down.

In the year 1782, Francis Leske, Esq was deputy governor of this Castle, with a salary of £91 5s per annum. It is subordinate to the garrison of Portsmouth.

The shore of Southsea Beach is the daily resort of company, and is frequented both morning and evening, where the sea breeze is very refreshing and salubrious, and the view from the sea at once extensive and delightful:

> Mark the surrounding sea o'ershadow'd with our fleets;
> Behold yon ships that glide before the rising gale,
> With streamers glittering in the noon beam day.

It must also be observed that the sands are particularly firm after the waves have quitted them; that they are pleasant to the tread; and that no ill effects are here experienced from either damp air or soil; nor are parties in sailing excursions liable to take cold by having their feet, legs or clothes made wet by sea water.

There is also a safe place for open bathing along the Southsea beach, where the sea covers a fine gravelly bottom to the length of half a mile. There are also convenient bathing machines fitted up and ranged along the shore; as the company which have for late years frequented Southampton are rapidly diminishing, we may naturally conclude that sea bathing at Portsmouth will increase in proportion; indeed, it is rather a matter of surprise that Southampton should ever have had the preference in this respect to Portsmouth, for surely when the shores are laved by the sea in all its saline strength, it must be preferable to a place like Southampton, where it is mixed with fresh water and by this means considerably weakened in its salutary effects on such as bathe for the recovery of their health, strength, or spirits.

To young people, and particularly to children, sea bathing is of great importance. — Their lax fibres render its tonic powers peculiarly serviceable. It promotes their growth, increases their strength, and prevents a variety of diseases incident to childhood.

> Oh! recreation, exquisite to feel,
> The wholesome waters trickle from the head,
> Oft as its saturated locks emerge!
> To feel them lick the hand, and lave the foot!
> And when the playful and luxuriant limb
> Is satiate with pastime, and the man
> Rises refresh'd from the voluptuous flood,
> How rich the pleasure to let zephyr chill,
> And steal the dew-drops from his panting sides![97]

It is, however, necessary to caution young men against too frequent bathing and continuing in the water too long: every beneficial purpose is answered by one immersion at a time.[98]

Nearly three miles from Southsea Castle along the coast is Cumberland Fort, which the late Lord Tyrawley caused to be erected for the defence of this part of the coast. It mounts 100 pieces of ordnance and by secret passages the troops stationed there can act upon any angle of the fort without being annoyed by the enemy. And upon an emergency will contain upwards of 4,000 troops.

About three hundred yards from Landport gates, on the left, formerly stood a small chapel called *Magdalen Chapel*, dependent on one of the religious houses in the neighbourhood destroyed at the reformation; not many years since some traces remained of it.

---

97 [from "The Favourite Village" by James Hurdis]

98 Lately have been erected a reading room and bathing-house on Southsea beach, by subscription; the room is now finished. There are in it hot and cold baths.

On the right hand side of the London Road, near the half way houses, is a large and handsome edifice, the residence of the Commanding Engineer at this place; there are also several very spacious buildings and offices belonging to this department. Some of them have been very recently erected on the mill dam near Portsea. This town and its neighbourhood derive much beauty and convenience from the excellent order in which the department sustain the various works and roads belonging to it, and they have considerably improved and benefited the place by so doing.

In the neighbourhood of Portsmouth are many scattered hamlets and villages. The village of Kingston is both populous and pleasant; the parish church of Kingston is here situated. The structure is handsome and the style of the architecture, being plain and simple pointed arches without any ornament, indicates it to have been erected about the reign of Edward I. The burying ground which surrounds it is remarkable for its extent, but contains no particular monuments worthy of notice except one which is erected to the memory of the unfortunate sufferers in the Royal George, several of whose bodies, which floated ashore after the unhappy casualty, were interred in a large grave at the south east corner of the burial ground.

Buckland, another hamlet near Kingston, belonged, by *doomsday book,* to the family of the *De Ports,* as did another manor in the same hundred then called *Applestede,* which is supposed to have been afterwards called *Kingston.*

The estates of the *De Ports* became forfeited to the crown on the *attainder* of *John De Ports,* and I think that the two manors of Buckland and Applestede were given afterwards, as escheats of the crown, about the latter end of the reign of John, to the Corporation of Portsmouth, or as it was then expressed *"ad Homines de*

Portesmue[99]."

On the right of the London Road, near Hilsea, is Gatcombe house, the residence of Sir Lucius Curtis; this edifice is supposed formerly to have been a monastery; several human skulls have been dug up here at different periods which tend to corroborate the assertion; however there are no historical traces whatever known of it, except that by an inquisition taken in the second year of the reign of Henry VIII, it appears that *John Bremshot* Esq died in the eighth year of the reign of Edward IV, (1450) seized with the Manor of Bremshot in the Isle of Wight, certain lands called *Little Gatcombe*, and twenty-two acres of land in the Island of Portsea, in the county of Southampton.

Near Gatcombe are Hilsea Barracks, large enough to receive two regiments of soldiers. They are only temporary and were built at the desire of his Royal Highness the late Duke of Cumberland for the reception of the troops that are to be embarked on any emergency for

---

99 It will not be improper to add a few particulars respecting the *family* of the *De Ports*.

Hugh De Port, was proprietor of the manor of St. John's house at *Warnford* in the reign of William the Conqueror.

Henry De Port his son, succeeded him, and was founder of the Priory of *Shireburne*; and was succeeded by,

Adam de Port, who in the year 1172, says *Hovedan, Calumniatus fuit de proditione regis; et quia ipse ad summonitionem regis stare judicio noluit exlegatus est ab Anglia.* He was however restored again to his rights, on paying 2000 marcs to the king.

William De Port his son, took his maternal grandmother's name, and signed himself *Willielmus de St. John, Filius et Hæres Adæ de Port,* and, in the 15th of King John, gave 500 marcs *regi* for livery of all the lands of *Adam de Port* his father; and in the 16th or 17th of John he executed the office of *Sheriff* of the county of Southampton.

foreign service.

At the distance of four miles from Portsmouth, the Island of Portsea communicates with the mainland over a large canal by a structure called *Portsbridge*. This canal, which unites Portsmouth and Langstone harbour, is widened and faced with stone in a manner that encreases the strength of this part of the fortifications.

About five miles from Portsmouth is *Portsdown Hill*, a narrow lofty eminence running east and west for nearly seven miles: the upper part of the *Stratum* consists of chalk broken into vast hollows, the lower part is brown loam. The prospects from its summits are of great extent and considerable variety. On the South, it commands a striking view of the British Channel, which is lost only in the *mist* of distance, with its majestic feature, the Isle of Wight, which is here seen through nearly its whole length. The dark blue tints of the New Forest mingle with the horizon in the West; on the North, the eye commands the extensive vale of the Forest of Bere; not as in ancient times, impervious and inaccessible, but agreeably interspersed with inclosures, cornfields and cottages;

> The spacious vale with flowers
> O'erspread, and copious herbage pleases at once
> The sight, and offers to the ready hand
> Spontaneous beauty ripening in the Sun![100]

And on the East the graceful spire of Chichester Cathedral appears rising above the level of the welds of Sussex. To enliven and animate the whole, multitudes of ships and vessels are seen navigating the channel, or remaining stationary in the harbour and Dockyard of Portsmouth.

---

100 [From Ogilvie's "Britannia"]

On the Eastern extremity of Portsdown Hill, a Telegraph was erected about twenty or thirty years ago; and an annual fair is held here on the 26th of July for the sale of goods, wearing apparel, grocery, wares, toys, and principally for horses, cheese, &c. which continues for three days.

Some labourers being employed in quarrying chalk during the month of September last, accidentally broke into a *tumulus* situated on the South side of the hill near the telegraph. The form of it appeared to be a parallelogram, extending East and West about 100 feet, in breadth about 20 feet, and in height 6 feet. In this *tumulus* or *Barrow* were discovered the remains of twelve bodies, some placed in *cists,* others laid only on the surface of the chalk, and covered by heaping the surrounding soil on them. The skeleton that was last discovered occupied a grave distinct from the others, but evidently too short for the stature of the person interred; loose flags were placed on it, their ends resting on the chalk. The *radius* and *ulna* were laid across the frame; the latter was the only bone entire, and was rather shorter than that of a well proportioned man. The *occipital* bone bore marks of petrifaction, and at the juncture of the *temporal* with the *parietal* bone, on the right side, was found inserted an iron head of a spear.

Numerous have been the conjectures respecting the *precise* time of the interment of the skeletons, but none of them have been in the least satisfactory. Some have supposed the *tumulus* to be *Roman,* but as those people generally burnt their dead and deposited their ashes in urns, and as no kind of utensils were discovered with the bodies, I am of opinion that they are mistaken. Others have imagined them to have been interred in the year 1142 during the Civil Wars of Stephen and Matilda, but there is not the least trace of any battle fought here to countenance the assertion; for when Matilda landed at

Portsmouth in 1139 she immediately threw herself into Arund Castle, and from thence retired to the City of Gloucester, leaving these maritime parts exempt from the miseries and horrors of civil war.

A late writer observes, "with regard to its being the cemetery of a *Belgie* village, I consider such opinion entirely fallacious. The bodies bear evident marks of violence, and in the disposing much haste has been made. But we do not find that the Belgæ formed their villages in such lofty and exposed situations; we trace them more frequently amid the sequestered shades of some deep forest; and such was, in the times alluded to, the situation of Porchester, seated on the margin of a vast and gloomy ardenne, as the records of much later ages sufficiently declare."

The most probable supposition is that they were interred during the times of the Danes and Saxons, in whose wars they might have lost their lives; as strong proof of their having been slain in battle is the circumstance of the iron head of a spear being found in one of the skulls; but as our island was thrown into the utmost confusion from the predatory warfare of the Danes, it cannot be a matter of surprise to any one that no historical relation of this engagement should be handed down to us, and the barbarism of the times and the total absence of literature not a little contributed to involve the annals of those times in obscurity.

Although Mr. Turner in his history of the Anglo Saxons has rescued many battles from oblivion, does it follow that "some relation would, without doubt have been handed down?" — On the contrary we must conclude that many battles must have been fought on these maritime parts, which have never been recorded by historians, particularly as the inhabitants were then incessantly engaged in warfare with the ferocious invaders. On the whole the subject is involved in great obscurity, and unless it may be in the power of some one to throw *greater* light on the history of those early times than has been done at present, I am clearly of opinion that it is *utterly impossible* to state with *any* degree of accuracy or truth the period of their interment.

About two miles distant from Portsdown Hill is the village of Purbrook; in the neighbourhood of which are some handsome houses which tend to embellish and enliven the scene.

Fareham, pleasantly situated at the head of Portsmouth Harbour, is a neat little town. In Doomsday Book, this place is mentioned as having been, by its maritime situation, exposed to the incursions of the Danes; who were for a long time the terror of the British coasts. At a short distance from the town is Cams Hall, an agreeable residence, the property of the *Delme* family.

Havant is a neat and respectable town situated at the eastern extremity of Portsdown Hill, consisting principally of one long street, crossed by another at right angles. Here in the morning of the 25th of October 1734, a shock of an earthquake was felt which continued for the space of two or three minutes; and after a short intermission, another shock, which lasted a similar space of time was also experienced: no damage was done, but the tremulous motion that accompanied the shocks spread great alarm. The number of houses in this town, as returned in 1801, was 345; that of inhabitants, 1670: the latter are chiefly supported by fowling and fishing. The market was granted by King John, probably through the intercession of the Monks of Winchester, to whom the manor was granted by Ethelred.

The Church is dedicated to St. Faith, and stands in the centre of the town; it is cruciform, with a tower rising from the intersection. The columns of the nave are of Saxon architecture; the arches are pointed. The windows of the north aisle having been of painted glass, seem a testimony of there having been there a private oratory. At the extremity of the other aisle, under a handsome niche, appear to have been deposited the remains of the founder of it. Above the tomb is a frail memorial of a mutilated image, the inscription (if any there ever was), has been long since defaced and rendered illegible by the initials of names inserted by idle visitors. In the wall of the south transept are some remains of stone seats.

The whole building displays specimens of the styles of different periods.

About two miles further under Portsdown, lies the pleasant village of Southwick; near it on the right is a large ancient mansion called Southwick Place, formerly the seat of Richard Norton, Esq, who in the reign of Charles I espoused the side of parliament. It was once a religious house, but suppressed among the others by King Henry VIII when the last prior, whose name was Norton, surrendered it to the King on an annual pension, and probably a grant of the priory from the King or his commissioners, as it remained long afterwards in the Norton family.

It came afterwards to Francis Whitehead, Esq; and at his death, to the family of the present Mr. Thistlethwayte. Oliver Cromwell had a great friendship for the ancestor of Richard Norton, which is evinced in the following letters addressed to him:—

"Deere Norton,

"I have sent my sonn over to thee beinge willinge to answere providence, and although I confesse I have had an offer of a very great proposition from a father of his daughter, yett truly I rather encline to this in my thoughts, because though the other bee very farr greater, yett I see different tyes, and not that assurance of godliness, yett indeed fairness. I confesse that which is tould mee concerning estate of Mr. M is more then I can looke for as thingss now stand.

"If God please to bring it about, the consideration of pietye in the parents, and such hopes of the gentlewoeman in that respect make the businesse to me a greate mercy, concerning wch I desier to waite upon God.

"I am *confident* of thy love, and desier thinges may be carried with privacie. The Lord doe his will, that's best, to wch submitinge I rest your humble servant.

"O. CROMWELL.

"February, 25, 1647

"For my noble friend Col.

"Richard Norton, theise."

"Deere Dick,

"Itt had beene a *favour* indeed to have met you heere at Farnham, but I heere you are a man of great *business.* — Therefore I say noe more, if it be a favour to the House of Commons to enjoy you, what is itt to me? But in good earnest when will you and your brother Russell be a *little* honest and attend your charge suerly some expect itt, especially the good fellowes who chose you.

"I have met wth Mr. Maior, wee spent two or 3 howers together last night. I perceave the gentleman is very wise and honest, and indeed much to be vallewed, some thinges of comon fame did a little sticke, I gladly heard his doubts, and gave such answare as was next att hand, I believe to some satisfaction, neverthelesse I exceedingly liked the gentlemen's plainesse, and free dealinge wth mee. I know God has been above all ill reports, and will in his own time vindicate mee, I have noe cause to complaine. I see nothinge but that this particular businesse betweene him and mee may go onn. The Lord's will be done. For newes out of the north there is little, only the Mal.

partye is prevailing in the Parlnt. of S. They are earnest for a warr, the ministers oppose as yett.

"Mr. Marshall is returned, whoe sayis soe. And soe doe many of our letters, their great committee of dangers have 2 malig. for one right. Its sayd they have voted an armie of 40,000 in parlnt. soe some of yesterdayes letters, but I account my newes *ill* bestowed, because upon an *idle* person.

"I shall take speedy course in the businesse concerning my tenants, for wch thankes, my service to your lady, I am really

"Your affectionate Servant,

"O CROMWELL."

"March 28 1648.

    "Farnham.

"For my noble friend Col.

Richard Norton, theise."

"Deere Norton,

"I could not in my last give you a perfect account of what passed between me and Mr. M. because wee were to have a conclusion of our speed that morninge after I wrote my letter to you, which wee had, and havinge had a full enterview of one another's mindes, wee parted with this, that both would consider with our relations, and accordinge to satisfactions given there, acquaint each other with our mindes.

"I cannot tell how better to doe itt, to receave or give satisfaction then by *you*, whoe (as I remember) in your last, sayd that if thinges did stick betweene us, you would use your endeavour towards a close.

"The thinges insisted upon were theise, (as I take itt.) Mr. Maior desired 400 *p. annum* of inheritance lyinge in *Cambridgesheire* and

Norfolke, to bee preasently settled, and to be for maintenance, wherein I desired to be advised by my wife.

"I offered the land in *Hampshire*, for present maintenance, wch I dare say with copses and ordinarie fells will be *communibus annis* £500 *p. annum*, besides £500 *p. annum*, in tennants handes houldinge but for one life, and about £300 *p. ann.* some for two lives, some for three lives. But as to this if the latter bee not liked off, I shall bee willing a farther conference bee had in the first.

"In point of jouncture I shall give satisfaction. And as to the settlement of landes given mee by the parlnt. satisfaction to be given in like manner, accordinge as wee discoursed.

" In what else was demanded of mee, I am willinge (soe far as I remember any demand was) to give satisfaction.

"Only I havinge beene enformed by Mr. Robinson, that Mr. Maior did upon a former match offer to settle the mannor wherein hee lived, and to give £2000 in monie, I did insist upon that, and doe desire it may not bee with difficultye, the monie I shall neede for my *two little wenches*, and therby I shall free my sonn from beinge charged with them. Mr. Maior parts wth nothing in præsent but that monie, savinge their board, wch I should not bee unwillinge to give them to enjoy the comfort of their societye, wch itts reason hee smarte for, if hee will rob mee altogether of them. Truly the land to bee settled both what the parlnt gives mee, and my owne is very little lesse than £3000 *per annum*, all things considered, if I bee rightly informed. And a *lawyer*, of Lincoln's Inn havinge searched all the marques of Worcester's writinges, wch were taken at Ragland, and sent for by the Parlnt. and this gentleman appointed by the comittee to search the sayd writinges, assures mee, there is noe scruple concerninge the title, and itt soe fell out that this *gentleman* whoe searched was my owne *lawyer*, a *very godly* able man, and my deere friend, wch I reckon noe small mercy, hee is also possest of the writinges for mee.

"I thought fitt to give you this account, desiringe you to make such use of itt as God shall direct you, and I doubt not but you will doe the part of a friend betweene two frendes, I account *myself* one, and I have heard you say Mr. Maior was entirely soe to you. What the good pleasure of God is I shall write, there is only rest, present my service to your lady, to Mr. Maior, *et,*

"I rest

" Your affectionate servant,

"O. CROMWELL

"April the 3d, 1648"   .

"I desier you to carrie this business with all privacie, I beseech you to doe soe *as you love mee,* let me entreat you not to loose a day herein, that I may knowe Mr. Maior's minde, for I thinke I may be att leisure for a weeke to attende this businesse to give and take satisfaction, from wch perhaps I may bee shutt up afterwards by imployment. I know thou art an *idle fellowe,* but prethee neglect mee not now, delay may bee very inconvenient to mee, *I much rely upon you.* Lett me here from you in two or 3 days. I confesse the principall consideration as to mee is the absolute settlement of the mannor where he lives, wch he would doe but conditionally in case he prove to have noe sonn, and but £3000 in case he have a sonn. But as to this, I hope farther reason may work him to more."

In the ancient history of this place, *Humphrey Lord Stafford* was, in the reign of King Edward IV stiled *Lord Stafford of Southwick.*

The Priory of Southwick was originally established at *Porchester*

by Henry I in the year 1133, but was not long after removed to
Southwick, where it continued to flourish till the Dissolution. Its
privileges were extensive; and in 1235, the *Canons* procured the
grant of a *market* and a *fair* to be held here, but the former has been
disused: they also obtained liberty of free warren in the year 1321. At
the Dissolution the annual revenues of this establishment were,
according to Dugdale, valued at £257 4s 4d, but according to *Speed*,
at £314 7s 10d.

The scite and demesnes of the Priory were then granted to John
White, Esq and Catherine his wife, who lye interred in the chancel of
Southwick Church, with the following inscribed on the tomb:

*"Here resteth in peace ye body of John White Esquyer, fyrst
owner of ye priorie and mannor of Southwick, att the surrender
and departyng of ye chanons from ye same, and Katyne hys Wiff,
ye only daughter of Willm. Pounde of Drayton, Esq. and Mary one
of ye daughter and hayres of Thomas Haynes of th' yle of Wight,
Esq. ye wh Katyne deceased ye laste day of October, An. Dni. 1541,
and ye sayd John deceased ye xix daye of Julie, An Dni. m,ccccc,
lxvii, whos soule take to hys mercye, Amen."*

From them it descended by the female line to Col. Norton, who
signalized himself in behalf of the Parliament during the Civil Wars,
and whose family had long resided at Southwick, in great
respectability.

His grandson Richard, the last male heir, was celebrated for his
extraordinary will, by which he bequeathed Southwick and all his
other estates to the amount of £6000 *per annum*, together with
personal property, to the value of £60,000 to the *parliament* of
Great Britain, in trust, for the use of *"the poor, hungry, thirsty,*

naked strangers, sick, wounded, and prisoners, to the end of the world." The will was, however, set aside from the very evident marks of insanity that appeared to have dictated its clauses.

The Chapel of the *Priory* is still worthy the attention of the visitor. Its venerable appearance is rendered very impressive by fourteen beautiful *gothic* windows on each side. In the south wall is a curious niche with a flight of stone steps leading to it, which justifies the conjecture of its having been formerly the *pulpit* belonging to the priory. The *cells* of the canons beneath this room are now the depositories of *fire-wood*. In the church-yard of *Southwick* is the following *singular* epitaph:

In Memory

of

William Lewis,

Who departed this Life the 21 st of October, 1763,

aged 80.

Here Lewis the brave,

That ne'er was a slave,

Tho' Norton the great,

Drove him to fate;

He returns here to rest,

Like Norton the great;

O men would be Gods!

Southwick is also remarkable, from its having been the scene of the *Marriage of Henry VI* with *Margaret of Anjou*[101]. Here it was

---

101 A curious picture of these nuptials, was engraved to illustrate Walpole's Anecdotes of Painting. *Kemp*, Archbishop of York, is represented holding the *pallium* over the joined hands of *Henry* and *Margaret*;

that Charles I came, when he accompanied his favourite, *Villiers, Duke of Buckingham*, then going to embark at *Portsmouth* on his second expedition against the French; and here he received the melancholy news of the *Duke* having been assassinated by the hand of *Felton*.

---

among;the attendants are *Cardinal Beaufort*, and the *Dukes* of *Gloucester* and *Suffolk*.

CHAPTER VIII

Of the Isle of Wight[102].

THIS Island has, for picturesque beauty, been considered equal to any spot of its extent in the kingdom. The form of it is an irregular lozenge, measuring nearly twenty three miles from the eastern to the western angle and fourteen from the northern to the southern.

It is about sixty miles in circumference and it comprises 105,000 acres.

The face of the country is beautifully diversified and the soil highly productive. The water is generally good; in some places the springs have been found to be impregnated with minerals. One in particular, a very powerful aluminous chalybeate has been discovered near Niton.

The farms in the island are moderate in size; few under £100 a year, and some under £600; but in general somewhat between these sums. Timber, which in the reign of Charles II was so plentiful here that it is said a squirrel might then have travelled on the tops of the trees for many successive miles, is not at present very abundant. The greater part of its flourishing woods have long since found a market at Portsmouth Dock.

Game is very plentiful: for neither fox, badger nor polecat was ever known in this island. Henry VIII was so intent upon preserving the game from poachers that in the year 1541 he addressed to R. Worsley Esq, captain of the island, a mandate directing him, "to have

---

102 Those who are desirous of obtaining more information respecting this very beautiful spot of ground, are requested to refer to *John Bullar's* historical and picturesque guide to the Isle of Wight, from which the following account is principally taken.

diligent regarde and vigilant eye that no man of no degree or condition, kill any fesant or partriche with net, engyne, or hawk, on any our propre lands, in the same isle; taking the netts and engyns of all such as shall attempt the contrary, and further punisheng the parties soe offending, as to your wisdom shall be thought convenyent."

The natural fortifications of this island in many places are rocks and lofty cliffs; where these are wanting, government has supplied forts and blockhouses.

The climate is mild and salubrious, but from the numerous hills attracting the vapours, there are frequent rains.

The coasts yield all kinds of fish, and among them may be reckoned the lobster and crab of peculiar excellence and size.

The early history of the Isle of Wight is involved in darkness, similar to that of the larger island of which it is an appendage.

Vespasian was the first who planted the Roman standard in this island during the reign of Claudious, A.D. 43. During the whole time that the Romans possessed this district, for the space of four-hundred years, we read of no disturbance on the part of the conquered, nor of any severity on that of the victors. The population was probably very scanty and therefore easily kept under subjection.

To the mild and civilizing sway of the Romans, succeeded the dominion of the furious and devastating Saxons; who obtained possession of the Island in 530.

At the death of Cerdic in 534, it devolved to his nephews, Withgar and Stuffa. These bloody chieftains are said to have actually murdered all the inhabitants who had survived the persecutions of their uncle.

In 661 it was attacked and laid waste by Wulpher, King of Mercia; who presented it to Edelwalch, King of the South Saxons, under whom it continued till 686; when Cadwalla, a lineal descendant of Cerdic and King of Wessex, destroyed Edelwalch and annexed it to his own dominions.

On the conquest of England 1066, by William the Norman, that monarch bestowed the island on William Fitz-Osborne, to be held by him as freely as the king himself held the realm of England. Fitz-Osborne having lost his life four years after on the continent, the Isle of Wight descended to his third son Roger de Breteville, Earl of Hereford. This Baron having been concerned in a conspiracy to depose the king, was condemned to perpetual imprisonment, and the island escheated to the crown. His spirits, however, remained unbroken by his sufferings; for at a solemn celebration of the feast of Easter, the king having sent him his robes, to show his contempt of what was doubtless meant as a compliment, he burnt them. Which being told the king, he vowed with an oath that the earl should spend the remainder of his life in confinement. He died in prison, A.D. 1086.

From the time of William the Conqueror to the 23rd of Edward I[103], the island seemed to have enjoyed a state of tranquillity; but at that time the coast of England was threatened with a descent, and a numerous fleet being fitted out by France, Edward, who had then purchased the lordship of the Isle of Wight, appointed the Bishop of Winchester, Adam de Gordon, and Sir Richard de Affeton for its defence, joining them in commission as wardens, and giving them instructions and orders for their conduct in case of an attack; no attempt, however, appears to have been made on it at that time. It continued unmolested till the 13th year of Edward III[104]; during whose contest for the crown of France the enemy landed at the

---

103 [1295]
104 [1340]

eastern extremity of the Island in considerable numbers: they were warmly opposed by the wardens and inhabitants and were obliged to retire with loss to their shipping.

Early in the reign of Richard I[105], the French landed with considerable force, proceeded into the interior, and attacked Carisbrook Castle. It was gallantly defended by Sir Hugh Tyrrel, and the invaders were obliged to retire; but not until they had extorted from the inhabitants a contribution of 1000 marks.

In the fifth year of Henry V[106], a large party of French landed for the purpose, as they said, of keeping Christmas. Their entertainment, however, was a sorry one; for they were repulsed with great loss.

In the 36th of Henry VIII, D'Annebant[107], the French admiral, landed 2000 men in three different parts of the island. Their intention was to take possession, and fortify it for the King of France. But Richard Worsley, captain of the island, coming upon them, drove them to their ships with the loss of the admiral and great part of his forces.

In the civil wars of the seventeenth century, Colonel Robert Hammond had the command of the island, who presided in the castle during the whole of the imprisonment of Charles I. From which time the history of the Isle of Wight happily ceases to afford any further military anecdotes of any particular consequence.

Newport, the capital of the island, and conveniently situated nearly in its centre, is a pleasant and populous town. It is regularly built and has handsome shops and good inns. The markets are held on Wednesdays and Saturdays; 200 waggons, loaded with different grain, have frequently been brought here on a market day; their

---

105 [Richard I came to power on 3rd September 1189]

106 [March 21st, 1417 to March 20th, 1418]

107 [April 22nd, 1544 to April 21st, 1545]

contents amounting to fourteen or fifteen hundred quarters, great part of which is manufactured in the island into flour, malt, and biscuit for the use of the navy.

Of the buildings, appropriated for divine service, the Church necessarily demands our chief attention. It is of great antiquity, but like all places where time has committed its ravages, it is indebted to various additions and repairs for its present appearance. It stands in the centre of one of the squares of the town and consists of a nave and two side aisles with a square tower. The chancel is divided from the body of the church by small oak pillars and arches, ornamented with carving. The pulpit is a curious relic of antiquity, of wainscot, richly ornamented with fourteen emblematic figures disposed in two rows in the different pannels round it, to represent the liberal sciences and cardinal virtues. The date is 1636.

The town of Newport was probably of very little importance till the reign of Henry II, as it seems to have been without a church till that time; this supposition is grounded on its church being dedicated to St. Thomas à Becket, the popular saint of that period, who was not canonized till the year 1172.

The first charter of immunities granted to this town, was from *Richard de Redvers*, Earl of Devon; its exact date is not known, but it must have been in the reign of Henry II, as this Earl died in the 30th year of that reign[108].

The Borough of Newport does not appear to have sent any members to parliament from the 23d of Edward I, until the 27th of Elizabeth[109], when many other boroughs, particularly all the boroughs in Hampshire, Southampton and *Portsmouth* excepted, received precepts each to send two burgesses to the parliament called

---

108 [December 19th, 1188 to July 6th 1189]

109 [1294 to 1585]

in that year.

By a Charter of Incorporation granted in the first year of James I[110], the Bailiff and Burgesses were Constituted a Body Politic, to consist of a Mayor, twenty-four Burgesses and a Recorder, with power to chuse a Town Clerk; the Mayor to be sworn into his office before the Captain of the Island or his Steward. The Mayor, Recorder, or his deputy, with two Burgesses, are impowered to hold a court every Friday, for the trial of all causes of debt, trespass, &c., arising within the Borough, according to the laws of England.

About a mile west from Newport, on a commanding eminence, stands the venerable ruins of Carisbrook Castle. The walls of the original fortress include about an acre and an half of ground, and are nearly in figure a rectangular parallelogram, having the greatest length from east to west.

The entrance is on the west side, over a bridge in a curtain between two bastions; then through a small gate, over which is a shield containing a date (probably that of its repair by Queen Elizabeth), from this by a passage having on each side an embattled wall, and under a very handsome machicolated gate, flanked with two round towers. The old door, with its wicket opening into the castle yard, is still remaining. It is formed of strong lattice work, having at each end a piece of iron, kept down by a strong nail. On the right is a small chapel; over the door is carved G. 2nd. 1738, and on the east end is a stone tablet, shewing that it was repaired during the government of Lord Lymington; at present there is no service performed in it.

Beyond this on the left hand, or north side, are several ruins of low buildings said to be those where Charles I, was confined; and in one of them is the window where he attempted his escape. Beyond

---

110 [1603]

these are the Barracks and the Governor's house. On the south-east angle, on a mount, raised considerably above the other buildings, is the Keep, an irregular polygon.

The ascent to it is by seventy-three steps, and on it are nine more. This place commands a most Delightful and extensive prospect. In this keep was formerly a well, said to have been 300 feet deep: but it is now partly filled up with rubbish, as being useless and dangerous.

In the north east angle stand the remains of another tower, called *Mountjoy's tower,* the walls of which are in many places eighteen feet thick. These towers have the appearance of much greater antiquity than the other buildings of the castle. The ramparts between the towers are about twenty feet high and eight feet thick; in both these dimensions is included the parapet, which formerly ran all round the works: it is but two feet and an half in thickness.

Nothing certain can be said as to the age of this castle. It is highly probable that both the ancient Britons and the Romans availed themselves of this advantageous situation; but however that may have been, no part of the present building can lay claim to such high antiquity.

It is said to have been re-edified in the reign of Henry I[111] by *Richard de Redvers,* one of the lords of the island; so that according to this account it must have been built considerably before that time, to have stood in need of repairs. It was likewise much repaired in Queen Elizabeth's time.

Baldwin de Redvers, one of those barons who took up arms against king Stephen, being driven from his castle at Exeter, shut himself up in this fortress. Stephen, however, soon attacked him and took the castle at the first assault. Baldwin found means to escape, and died in exile.

---

111 [1154-1189]

Carisbrook castle was used by Oliver Cromwell and Charles II as a prison.

Carisbrook village had formerly a convent of Cistertian Monks, on the site of which stands a farm called the Priory.

About five miles from Newport stands *Quarr Abbey*; but a few vestiges of the abbey church, some cellars, and the refectory are nearly all its present remains. The wall which surrounded it in the days of its splendour was nearly a mile in circumference, as may still be traced. The situation is pleasingly secluded, being sheltered with woods, except where it opens to the sea.

This monastery was a convent of Cistertians founded by Baldwin, Earl of Devon, in the 32nd year of Henry I, and named the Abbey of Quarr, probably from the neighbouring quarries. After the Dissolution, the materials of the buildings were purchased by a person of Southampton, who carried great part of them, without respect to the sepulchres of many persons of rank who were buried here. Among them were its founder, Earl Baldwin, Adeliza his Countess, and Henry their son; the lady Cicely, second daughter of Edward IV, and William de Vernon, who bequeathed £300 (a vast sum in the thirteenth century), for the erecting of his monument. It has been well observed, that "nobody could say to a Norman baron, *immemor sepulchri, struis domos*[112]."

> "I do love these ancient ruins:
> We never tread upon them but we set
> Our foot upon some reverend history,
> And questionless, here, in this open court,
> Which now lies naked to the injuries
> Of stormy weather, some men lie interr'd

---

112 ["Forgetful of the tomb, you build houses"]

Loved the church so well, and gave so largely to 't,
They thought it should have canopy'd their bones
Till doomsday. But all things have an end.
Churches and cities, that have diseases like to men,
Must have like death that we have."[113]

Ryde is a place of some consequence as being one of the visual communications with Portsmouth, distant about eight miles. It is divided into *Upper* and *Lower*, being partly built on a pleasant eminence with a fine command of prospect towards Portsmouth and Gosport.

This place is in a state of rapid improvement; although even a few years ago it was no more than an insignificant village it begins now to assume the appearance of a town of some importance. One of the most important improvements of Ryde will be the pier; for the erection of which an Act of Parliament has been obtained. The object of this pier is to remedy the inconveniences of embarking and disembarking. Earl Spencer has lately erected a mansion on the west side of the town, which commands noble views of Spithead, Portsmouth, and the opposite coast.

The fine open situation of Ryde as a summer residence; its convenient distance from the metropolis; its good and safe sea-bathing and the purity of the sea-water; its conveniences for the most agreeable land and water excursions in the midst of scenery not easily to be paralleled for beauty and variety can scarcely fail to raise its estimation with the public, and ultimately, to render it the rival of the most popular summer resorts in the kingdom.

There are passage vessels between this place and Portsmouth, both morning and afternoon; and at the same parts of the day,

---

113 [From "The Duchess of Malfi," by John Webster]

coaches run to and from Newport.

At the distance of half a mile from Ryde, towards the left, is *Apley*, the seat of Captain Hutt.

Brading, a small market town, has nothing very remarkable in it. The first religious establishment in the island is said to have been at this place. The present church is ancient and there are in it some old monuments of the Oglanders. Its tower stands singularly on four open arches, which form a porch to the west door. This town formerly sent members to parliament, but was excused from so doing, by reason of the inability of its inhabitants to pay their representatives.

Niton is situated in a hollow, ornamented with fine trees, about six miles from Newport, and though within a mile of the sea, the coast is higher than the village and shelters it from the breezes of the sea. A rill of water runs through it. The parsonage is a neat residence, built by the Rev. Mr. Barwis, the present incumbent. The church is of great antiquity. The cross on the south, standing without the wall that encloses the church yard, raised with large hewn stones, placed in the manner of steps, with a basin at the top, manifestly designed for the purpose of baptism, prior to the use of fonts in churches, demonstrates its very ancient date. The church of Niton was given by Charles I with others in Hampshire to Queen's College, Oxford, in exchange for the college plate. In the register is recorded the landing of Charles II in 1675 at Southampton after a dangerous storm. Near it are ruins of Wolverton chapel, built by Ralph de Wolverton, A.D. 1370.

At Burton, near West Cowes, was a Priory of Austin Canons, as early as the reign of Edward I. But in the year 1275, this house was made a college or *oratory*, dedicated to the Holy Trinity, for a society of priests under the government of an archpriest. They gave their lands to St. Mary's College, Winchester, in the reign of Henry VI.

West Cowes, the principal port of the island, stands on the declivity of a hill, at the mouth of the river Medina. Its first appearance on landing is apt to give no very favourable impressions to the visitor; but it is pleasant and airy and is very convenient for sea bathing at any time of the tide in commodious machines placed on the beach. The neighbourhood of Cowes, with its extensive sea prospects, is highly pleasant and even preferable to the neighbourhood of Newport. Westward of the castle is the seat of Sir Thomas Tancred, Baronet, delightfully situated on the shore. The town has three good inns, many lodging houses, and a circulating library. The Marine Hotel is very pleasantly situated not far distant from the castle with a good sea view.

Cowes Harbour, from its safety and convenience, is much frequented by shipping; particularly in time of war by merchant vessels waiting for convoy.

On the opposite side of the river, over a short ferry, is the smaller town called *East Cowes*. On a hill behind the town, Lord Henry Seymour has erected a dwelling house on the plan of a castle; which is allowed by competent judges to be very fine in general outline, but not altogether correct in the detail of the style intended to be followed. There are also near this several other handsome residences; among which the castellated villa of J. Nash Esq excites particular notice.

Shanklin is a chapelty to Brading. In the church is a carved oak chest, inscribed **dompnus Thomas Silksted, Anno Domini 1512, T.S.** and the Arms of the See, being the gift of the prior of Winchester, who has a chapel in his Cathedral. — The situation of the *Chine,* as it is called, at a small distance from the village, is exceedingly romantic; a prodigious fissure of the rock on the south east coast of the island running a considerable way into the land, overgrown with shrubs and bushes and forming a beautiful and picturesque scene. The path down to the sea is very steep and half way down is a fisherman's cottage in a beautiful and secluded spot.

The neat little town of Yarmouth stands on a bank sloping to the sea in an airy situation, with pleasant views of the channel and of the coast of Hampshire. It is a borough, and has regularly sent members to parliament from the 27th of Elizabeth[114]. It obtained a Charter of Franchises from Baldwin de Redvers in the thirteenth century and was re-incorporated by King James I in the seventh year of his reign. The castle was erected by Henry VIII. The church stands in the middle of the Town. In a small chapel adjoining to it is a handsome monument of Admiral Sir R. Holmes, who was made Governor of the island in 1667 and died in 1692. It is called Yarmouth from its situation at the mouth of the Yar or Yare; in the ancient charters it is called *Eremuth*, and is the first town in the island which obtained a charter of franchises in the reign of Henry III.

Yarmouth is much diminished from its ancient consequence; its many narrow streets, destitute of buildings at present and laid out methodically in right angles, clearly point out its formerly more enlarged scite. There is a custom still retained here (peculiar to this place only, and not common in other parts of the kingdom) of the children's singing on New Year's day, *wassall* or *wassail* from the *Saxon*, "Health to you."

> " Wassal, wassal, to our town!
> The cup is white, and the ale is brown,
> The cup is made of the ashen tree,
> And so is the ale of good barley;

---

114 [1584]

Little maid, little maid, turn the pin,
Open the door, and let me come in;
God be here, and God be there!
I wish you all a happy new year."

It is impossible to close this account of the Isle of Wight without making this observation, that such is the richness of the soil, such the plenty, variety and perfection of its produce, as well as pleasantness of situation, that it has been justly called the *Garden of England*: but as this spot is daily visited by numbers of gentlemen and ladies of all ranks, we will neither echo nor anticipate the Judgment of others, but leave it to them to decide how well it deserves so great a character.

THE END

APPENDIX

No. 1
The Sowth Flete.
From an original MS preserved in the Library belonging to the
Dean and Chapter of Canterbury.

The Kinge,	{	Shipps xxv. Marriners ccccxix
Aileforde,	{	Shipps ii Marriners xxiv
Hoo,	{	Shipps ii Marriners xxiv
Maidstone,	{	Shipps ii Marriners li
Hope,	{	Shipps ii Marriners lix
Newhithe,	{	Shipps v Marriners xlix
Margate,	{	Shipps xx Marriners clx
Motne, or Mome,	{	Shipps ii Marriners xxiii
London,	{	Shipps xxv Marriners dclxii

Feversham,	{	Shipps ii Marriners liii
Sandwich,	{	Shipps xxii Marriners div
Dover,	{	Shipps xvi Marriners cccxxxvi
Wight,	{	Shipps xvi Marriners ccxx
Waymouth,	{	Shipps xx Marriners cclxiii
Lyme,	{	Shipps iv Marriners lxii
Seton,	{	Shipps ii Marriners xxv
Sydmouth,	{	Shipps iii Marriners lxii
Exmouth,	{	Shipps x Marriners cxciii
Tegmouth,	{	Shipps vii Marriners cxx
Dartmouth,	{	Shipps xxxi Marriners dcclvii
Portsmouth,	{	Shipps v Marriners xcvi

Plymouth,	{	Shipps xxvi Marriners dxiii
Loo,	{	Shipps xx Marriners cccxxv
Yalme,	{	Shipps ii Marriners xlvii
Iforvey,	{	Shipps xlvii Marriners dcclxx
Bristol,	{	Shipps xxii Marriners dcviii
Teinmouth,	{	Shipps ii Marriners xx
Hastings,	{	Shipps v Marriners xcvi
Romney,	{	Shipps iv Marriners lxv
Rye,	{	Shipps ix Marriners clvi
Hythe,	{	Shipps vi Marriners cxxii
Shoram,	{	Shipps xx Marriners cdxxix
Seford,	{	Shipps v Marriners lxxx
Newmouth,	{	Shipps ii Marriners xviii

Hanilhoke,	{	Shipps vii Marriners cxvi
Hoke,	{	Shipps xi Marriners ccviii
Sowthampton,	{	Shipps xxi Marriners dlxxvi
Leymington,	{	Shipps ix Marriners xciv
Poole,	{	Shipps iii Marriners lix
Warham,	{	Shipps iii Marriners lix
Swynsey,	{	Shipps i Marriners xxix
Ilfercombe,	{	Shipps vi Marriners lxxix
Patricksrow,	{	Shipps vi Marriners lx
Polereman,	{	Shipps i Marriners lx
Wadworth,	{	Shipps i Marriners xiv
Caerdiff,	{	Shipps i Marriners vii
Bridgewater,	{	Shipps i Marriners xv

Caermarthen,	{	Shipps i Marriners xvi
Cazlethsworth,	{	Shipps i Marriners vii
Mulbroke,	{	Shipps i Marriners vii
Some of the Sowth Flete,	{	Shipps cdlxxxiii Marriners ix dcxxx[115]

No. II

An order for arming the Clergy of the Isle of Wight, 12th Edward III[116], in consequence of the descents of the French on *Portsmouth*.

Adam &c. Official. Archidiaconi nostri Winton. sal. &c. Mandatum Dni Regis recipimus in hæc verba. Edwardus Rex Gr. &c. Adamo eadem Gr. Epo. Winton. Sal. &c. Quid quamplures Homines de Partibus et Dominiis Franciæ in diversis Galiis et Navibus super mare proficiscuntur regnum nostrum in partibus, de *Portesmuth* hostiliter invadentes, ac incendia depredationes et alia facinora quamplurima *ibidem* perpetrantes, et jam super mare versus *Insulam Vectam* se tenentes intentos mala et facinora consimilia vel pejora in eadem Insula et *aliis* locis regni nostri inhumaniter perpetrare nisi eorum malita celerius refrænatur. Ac nos volentes

---

115 The addition of the total amount is extremely incorrect, as is generally the case in all old accounts of this kind. The amount should be;

| Ships | cmlxxii | [986] |
| Marriners | ix cdlxv | [9,465] |

116 [That is, the year commencing January 25th, 1338]

defensioni et salvationi Regni nostri providere et horum hostilem nequitiam repellere Dno. annuente ac advertentes mala et pericula quæ ex hoc evenire poterant qd homines Ins. præd. tam viri Religiosi quam alii terras et possessiones in Insula præd. habentes et qui pro defensione et salvatione ejusdem tarn pro ipsorum quam nostro comodo et honore et sua exponere debent, se a dicta Insula hactenus elongarunt et retraxerunt, et ad hue elongant et retrahunt. Assignavimus dilectos fideles nostros lohem de Langford Custodem Castri nostri de Caresbrook in Insula præd. Barthol. de l'Isle, et Theobald. Russel et eorum quemlibet ad distrengond. et aliis viis et modis quibus poterunt compellend. omnes et singulos in Insula præd. commorantes vel terras tenentes seu alias possessiones in eadem.habentes alibi degentes qui ratione terrarum tenementorum et possessionum suarum ad defensionem ejusdem tenentur ad inveniend, homines ad arma, armatos Sagittarios et alios in dicta Insula pro defensione illius juxta quantitatem terrarum et possession, suarum quas ibidem habent contra dictorum inimicorum nostrorum incursus dum præd. pericula sic imminent, et prout temporibus Progenitorum in *guerrarum* commotionibus fieri consuevit, ad capiend. et seisend. in manum nostram terras, possessiones ac bona hominum prædictorum in eadem Insula, qui hos homines armatos ad arma Sagittarios et alios invenire debererit,et eos ad hoc recusarunt invenire &c. Teste meipso apud Westm. 22° April, Anno Regni nostri 12°.

Ex Registro Adam. de Orleton Epi.

Winton. A.D. 1339.

No. III

The names of all the King's Majesty's Shippes, Galleys, Pynasses, and Rowbarges, with their Tonnage and number of Soldiers, Mariners and Gunners, at *Portesmouth, 5 Jan. Edw. VI. primo*[117]:

Shippes.	Tons.	Soldiers.	Brass p.	Iron p.
The Petir	600	400	12	78
The Mathewe	600	300	10	121
The Jhesus	700	300	8	66
The Pauncy	450	300	13	69
The Great Barke	500	300	12	85
The Lesse Barke	400	250	11	98
The Murryan	500	300	—	53
The Shruce of Dawske	450	250	—	39
The Christoffer	400	246	2	51
The Trynitie Henry	250	220	1	63
The Swepe Stake	300	230	6	78
The Mary Willoughby	140	160	—	23

---

117 [1548]

GALLEYS

Shippes.	Tons.	Soldiers.	Brass p.	Iron p.
T'Anne Gallant	450	250	16	46
The Sallamander	300	220	9	40
The Harte	300	200	4	52
The Antelope	300	200	4	40
The Swallome	240	100	8	45
The Unycorne	240	140	6	30
The Jeannet	180	120	6	35
The Newbarke	200	140	5	48
The Greyhounde	200	140	8	37
The Teager	200	120	4	39
The Bulle	200	120	5	42
The Lyone	140	140	2	48
The George	60	40	2	26
The Dragone	140	120	3	42

PYNNACES

Shippes.	Tons.	Soldiers.	Brass p.	Iron p.
The Fawcone	83	55	4	22
The Black Pynnes	80	44	2	15
The Hynde	80	55	2	26
The Spannyshe	20	26	—	7

Shallope

The Hare	15	30	—	10

ROWBARGES

Shippes.	Tons.	Soldiers.	Brass p.	Iron p.
The Sonne	20	40	2	6
The Cloude in the Sonne	20	40	2	7
The Harpe	20	40	1	6
The Maidenheade	20	37	1	6
The Gellyflowre	20	38		
The Ostrege fether	20	37	1	6
The Rose Slipe	20	37	2	6
The Flower de Lewce	20	43	2	7
The Rose in the Sonne	20	40	3	7
The Port quilice	20	38	1	6
The Fawcon in the Fetherlock	20	45	3	8

No. IV

The *first* Charter of Incorporation granted by King Richard I. to the *Borough of Portsmouth*, A.D. 1194.

Ricardus dei gcia Rex Angliæ dux Normann' Aquit' Comes Andeg' Archiepis Epis Abbalibz Comitibz Baronibz Just' Vicecomitz Balliuiss. Ministri & omnibz fidelibz suis tocius træ syæ. salutem. Siatis nos retinuisse in manu' n'ram Burgu' nostru' de *Portesmues* cu' omnibz ad eu' ptinentibz & i eo stabilisse et dedisse & cocessisse *nundinas*_duraturas semel in. Anno p quindecim dies ad uincula sci Petri scil. Concessim' ecia' quod omnes homines nostri Angliæ Normann' Andeg' Pictauiæ Walliæ Scociæ & oim trar' nrar & aliar' veniant ad p'dictas nundinas & eant & redeant bn & i pace & heant omnes quietancias & libertates quas hent ad nundinas Wynton' vel Hoiland' vel alibi i t'ram nostra'. Concessimus ecia' quod Burgenses nri in eodm Burgo heant singulis ebdomadis ani vna die septimane die Jouis scil mercatu' cu' omnlbz libertatibz & libris consuetudinibz quas ciues nostri Wynton' vl Oxensi vl alii t'rar' nostrar' hent vl habere debeant. Concessimus ecia' quod p'dca *villa* de *Portesmues* & omnes Burgenses nri in ea & de ea tenentes quieti sint & iibi d' thelonio & pontagio & stallagio & tallagio & de Schiris & hund'ris de sectis Schirar' & hundred' & de summonicoibz & auxiliis vic' & s'uientium & plitis & querelis omnibz & de *Blodwita*[118] & de *Siche wita leerwita*[119] & de Wapentac[120] & de plito forestæ & de guardo & de

---

118 Blodwita is an *Amerciament* or *Fine* for drawing *Blood*.

119 *Leerwita*, is a *Mulct* upon him who corrupts a *Bondwoman* or upon a *Bondman* for the *Fornication* of his daughter.

120 Free from *Suit* and *Service* to the *Wapentake Court*, as before, from *Suit* and *Service* to the *County* or *Shire Court*, and *Hundred Courts*.

regardo forestæ[121] & de omnibz aliis secularibz exaccionibz tam P mare qm P t'ram vbicunq' ven'int in totam t'ram nostra'. **Quare** volumus & firmiter p'cipim' quod p'dicta *villa* de *Portesmues* & Burgenses nri in ea tenentes mansiones suas & possessiones heant & teneant cu' *thol & theam*[122] & *infangenetheof*[23] & *vtfangenetheof*[24] cu' omnibz libertatibz & libis consuetudinibz ita bri & in pace libe & quiete sicut ciues nri Wynton' vl Oxnes vl alii de tra nostra melius & libius & quiecius possessiones suas & Iibertates hent & tenent. Et prohibemus ne ponantur in plitum de aliquo tenement' eiusdtn villæ nisi cora' nobis & phibemus ne quis eos disturbet in aliquo sup foris fcuram n'ram. Hiis testibz. Willo de sce marie ecclia. Magro Pho. Ganfr' fil' petri. Roberto filio Rogi. Ganfr' de say. Willmo de Stagno. Willmo Mallum. Dat' p manu' Willi de longo campo epi Elien' Cancellar' nostri' apud *Portesmui* secundo die Maii Regni nri Anno quinto.

---

121 There were in the King's forests certain officers called *Regardatores*, now called Rangers; who often viewed and went about the forests, to see if any wood was cut, venison stolen, and other trespasses committed therein; which inspection was called a *Regard* as was likewise the *punishment* for such offences and trespasses.

122 *Thol* signifies an imposition or payment for things bought and sold in *Mercates*. *Theam*, a privilege to take and keep *bondmen, villans*, and *servants*, with their *posterity*, and to *sell* and *dispose* of their children, or *moveable* and immoveable goods at pleasure.

123 *Infangenetheof* is a liberty granted to try and judge & thief taken within the jurisdiction of the Borough.

124 *Vtfangenetheof* is a privilege to take a thief that fled, and bring him back to the place wherein the fact was committed, and there to try and judge him.

No. V

The Charter of *King John*, granted in the year 1201.

J. dei g'cia Rex Angliæ dns hibniæ dux Normann' Aquit' & Comes
Andeg' Archiepis Epis Abbatibz Comitibz; Baronibz Justic'
Vicecomitibz Balliius Ministris & omnibz fidelibz tocius t'ræ suæ,
salutem. Sciatis nos retinuisse in manu' nostra' Burgum nrm de
Portesmues cu' omnibz ad eu' ptinentibz & i eu' stablisse & dedisse &
cocessisse *nundinas* duraturas semel i Anno p quindecim dies
Aduincula sci Petri scil'. Concessimus ecia qd omnes homines nostri
Angliæ Normann' Andeg' Pictaur Walliæ Scociæ & omu' traru'
nostrar veniant ad p'dictæs nundinas & eant & redeant & bene & i
pace & heant: oies quietancias & libertates quas hent ad nundinas
Wynton' vl Hoiland' vel alibi in t'ram nostrar'. Concessiinus ecia'
quod burgenses nri i eodem Burgo heant singulis ebdomadis Anni
vna die septimane die Jouis scil' m' catu' cu' omnibz libertatibz &
libis consuetudiniibz quas Cuies nostri Wynton' vl Oxens vel alii trar'
nostrar' hent vl habere debeant. Concessimus ecia' quod p'dca *villa*
de *Portesmut'* & omnes Burgenses nri in ea & de ea tenentes quieti
sint & liberi de *Theloneo*[125] & pontagio[126] & passagio[127] & pedagio[128] &

---

125 *Theloneum* is the same, with toll.

126 *Pontagium*, is a *toll* paid for passage *over* bridges with horses,
carriages, &c. and *under* them, with boats, ships, &c

127 *Passage* is money paid by *passengers* at bridges, gates, &c. which
may be called *gate toll, bridge toll,* &c.

128 *Pedagium* is money given for passing on horseback or foot through
any part of the country.

paagio stallagio[129] & tallagio[130] & de Schiris & hundred' de sectis schirar' & hundror' & de sumonicibnibz & auxiliis vicecomitu' & s'uientu' & plitis & querelis omnibz & de Blodwita & sichwita & lerwita & de Wapentac' & de plito forestæ & de gardo & regardo forestæ & de omnibz aliis secularibz exaccionibz tam p mare qm p t'ram vbicumqz venerunt in totam t'ram nostra' **Quare** volum' & firmiter p'cipimus quod p'da *villa* de *Portesmut'* & Burgenses nostri in ea tenetes mansiones suas & possessiones heant & teneant cu' thol & theam & infangenetheof & vtfangenetheof & cu' libtatibz & libis consuetudinibz ita bin & i pace libere & quiete sicut Cives nostri Wynton' vl Oxens vl alii de t'ra nostra melius & libius & quiecius possessiones suas & libertates hent & tenent. Et phibemus ne ponatur in plitum de aliquo tenemet' eiusdm villæ nisi cora' nobis vl capitali Justic' nro. Et phibemus ne quis eos disturbet in aliq° sup forisfcuram nostra' sicut carta Regis Rici fratris nostri racionabiliter testatur excepto h° quod additur in clausula vbi dicitur i carta Regis Ricardi no ponantur in plitum de aliq° tenemeto ejusdem' villæ nisi coram nobis ibi nos apposuimus vl capitali Justic'. T' Ganfr' fil petri. Com. Essex. 'W. Brew'. Rob' de Gurneham.— Hug' de.Neuill. Dat' p manu' Simon' Archid' Wellen apud *Melkesham* vicesimo quinto die' Octobr' regni nri Anno secundo.

No.VI

Charter of *King Henry III*, granted in the year 1230.

Henricus dei gracia Rex Angliæ dominus Hibniae Dux Normann' Aquit' & Comes Andeg' Archiepis Epis Abbatibz Prioribz Comitibz

---

129 *Stallage* is the privilege of erecting *stalls* in fairs or markets; also the money paid for the same.

130 *Tallagium* is a general word for all kinds of taxes.

Baronibz Justic' forestaræVicecomitibz P'positi s Ministris & omnibz Balliuis & fidelibz suis salutem. Siatis nos concessisse & hac carta nostra confirmasse hominibz nostris de *Portesmut'* nundinas in villa nostra de Portesmuth .duraturas semel in Anno p quindecim dies Aduincula sci petri scil'. Concessimus ecia' quod omnes homines nri Angliæ Normann' Andeg1 Pictauiæ Walliæ Scociæ & oim t'rar nostrar' & aliarum veniant ad p'dcas nundinas & eant & redeant it bn & i pace & heant omnes acquietancias & libertates quas hent ad nundinas *Wyntonniæ* vl Hoyland vl alibi i t'ra nra. Concessimus ecia' quod Burgenses nri in eodm Burgo heant singulis ebdomadis anni vna die septimane die Jouis scil' m'catu' cu' omnibz libertatibz & libis consuetudinibz quas Ciues nostri Wynton' vl Oxens' vl alii trar' nostrar' hent vl here debeant. Concessim1' ecia' quod p'dca villa de Portesmuth & oes Burgenses nri in ea & de ea tenentes quieti sint & libri de theloneo & pontagio & passagio & pedagio & paagio & stallagio & tallagio & de Schiris & hundris de sectes Schirar' & hundredor' & de summonicomibz & auxiliis vic' & s'uientium & plitis & querelis omnibz & de Blodwita & de sichwita & leerwita & de Wapentac' & de plito forestæ & de guardo & de reguardo forestæ & de omnibz aliis secularibz exacconibz tam p mare qm p tram' vbicumqz ven' int in tota' t'ram nostram. **Quare** volumus & firmiter p' cipim' quod p' dca *villa de Portesmuth* & Burgenses nostri in ea tenentes mansiones suas & possessiones heant & teneant cu' thol & theam & infangenetheof & vtfangenetheof & cu' omnibz libertibz & libis consuetudinibz ita bene & i pace libe & quiete sicut Ciues nostri Wynton' vl Oxens vl alii de t'ra nostra melius & liberius & quiecius possessiones suas & libertates hent & tenent. Et phibemus ne quis eos disturbet in aliquo sup forisfcuram nostra' sicut carta Ricardi Regis Avunculi nostri qm inde hent racionabiliter testatur. Hiis testibz Huberto de Burgo Com Kanc' Justic' nostro. Stepho de Segne.

Radulpho de Trublenill. Petro fil Herberti. Gillebto Basset. Godefrido de Crancumb'. Johanne fil Phi. Ricardo fil' Hugonis. Henrico de Capella & aliis. Dat p manu' Radi Cicest' Ep Cancellarii nostri apud *Wudestok* decimo octavo die Nouembris. Anno regni nostri quartodecimo.

No. VII
Another Charter, A. D. 1255.

Henricus dei gracia Rex Angliæ dominis hibniæ Dux Normann' Aquit' & Comes Andeg'. Omnibz Bailiuis'& fidelibz suis ad quos p'sentes Iræ peruen' int salutem. Siatis quod volumus & cocedimus p'nobis & heredibz nostris quod omnes libertates contentæ & exp'ssæ in cartis dominor' Ricardi regis avunculi nostri Johis regis. patris nostri & nostris quas Burgenses nri de *Portesmuth* hent tam de tallagiis qm aliis articulis de cetero teneantur & firmiter observentur secundu' quod iidem Burgenses hucusqz vsi sunt libtatibz p'dictis. In cuius Testiimoniu' has Iras nostras eisdm Burgensibz fieri fecim patentes. Teste me ipo apud *m'ton* quinto die Ap'l anno regni nri tricesimo nono.

No.VIII
Another Charter, A.D. 1256.

Henricus dei gcia Rex Angliæ domin' hibniæ dux Normann' Aquit' & comes Andeg' Archiepis Epis Abbatibz Prioribz Comitibz Baronibz Justic' Vicecomitibz P'positis Ministris & omnibz Balliuis & fidelibz suis salutem. Siatis nos concessisse & hac carta nra confirmasse *p'bis hominibz* nostris de *Portesmuth* quod ipi & eor' heredes inppetuu'

heant *Gildam M'catoria*[131] in p'dict' *villa de Portesmuth* cu' omnibz
libertatibz ad huiusmodi Gildam ptinentibz & quod ipi' & eor'
heredes inpetuu' p totam t'ram & potestatem nostra' habeant hac
libertertatem vz. quod ipi vel eor' bona quocumqz locoru' in potestate
nra inuenta non arestentur. p aliquo debito de quo fideiussores aut
principales debitores no' extit' int nisi forte ipi debitores de eor' sint
comuna & potestate hentes vnde de debitis suis in toto vl in parte
satisfac'e possint & dicti homines creditoribz eor' dem debitoru' in
iusticia defuerint & de hoc racionabiliter constare possit.
Concessimus ecia' eisdm hominibz quod inppetuu' quieti sint de
chemmagio[132] p forrestam nram sicut hucusqz quieti esse
consueverint. Et quod heant inter se tam in aquis portibz maris qm
in t'ris pascuis culturis & rebz aliis omnes Ieges & cosuetudines iustas
& approbatas & quietancias quas habuerut tepore dni J. Regis patris
nri & dni Ricardi Regis Auunculi nostri & alior' Antecessor' nostror'
Regu' Angliæ. **Quare** volum' & firmiter p'cipimus p'nobis & heredibz
nostris quod p'dict' homines de *Portesmuth* & eor' heredes inppetuur
heant predictam Gildam m'catoria'. Et quod heant inppetuu' omnes
libertates p'scriptas sicut p'dictu' e'. Et phibem' sup forisfcuram
nostra' decem librar' ne quis illos contra libertates ilias in aliquo
vexare aut inquietare p'sumat,. Hiis testibz ven'abilibz pat'bz W.
Elien' & W. Wigorn' Epis. Guidon' de lesimaco. Galfrido de lesimaco
& Willmo de Valencia fratribz nostris. Johe Maunsell. Thes' Eborac'
Willmo de Clara. Henrico de Bracton'. Nich' de turri. Walkelino de
Arderu'. Willmo de sancto Ermino, Bartholomeo le Bigot & aliis Dat'p
manu' nostra' apud *Clarendon'* quarto die Julii.. Anno regni nri
quadragessimo.

---

131 A Gild of Merchants was a *Trading Society* or a *Company of Buyers
and Sellers.*

132 *Chiminage* is a *toll* due for having a way through a forest.

Appendix

No. IX
Charter of *Confirmation* of *King Edward II*, A.D. 1313

Edwardus dei gracia Rex Angliæ domin' Hibniæ & Dux Aquit'
Archiepis Epis Abbatibz Prioribz Comitibz Baronibz Justic"
Vicecomitibz Prepositis Ministris & omnibz Balliuis & fidelibz suis,
salutem. Nos autem donaciones cocessiones & confirmacones p'dcas
ratas hentes & gratas eas p' nobis & heredibz' nostris qntu' i nobz &
p'fatis Burgensibz & eor' hedibz & successoribz Burgensibz villæ
p'dcæ concedim' & cofirmamus sicut Cartæ & Iræ patentes p'dcæ
racionabiliter testat'. Hiis testibz ven'abili patre W. Wygorn' Epo.
Gilberto de Clare Comite Gloucestre & herford. Hugone de Bello
Monte. Edmudo de malo laco Senescallo hospitii nri & aliis. Dat' p
manu' nostra' apud *Wyndesore* duodecimo die februarii Anni regni
nostri sexto.

No. X
Charter of *Confirmation* of *King Edward III*, A.D. 1359.

Edwardus dei gracia Rex Angliæ & franciæ & domin' Hibniæ
Archiepis Epis Abbatibz Prioribz Comitibz' Baronibz Justic'
Vicecomitibz P'positis Ministris & omnibz Balliuis & fidelibz suis
salutem. Nos autem donaciones concessiones & cofirmacones p'dcas
ratas hentes & g'tas eas p'nobis & heredibz nostris quantu' i nobz.&
p'fatis Burgensibz & eor' heredibz & successoribz Burgensibz villæ
p'dcæ concedim' & confirmamus sicut cartæ & Iræ patentes p'dcæ
racionabiliter testantur. Hiis testibz ven'abilibz patribz S. Archiepo
Cantuar' tocius Angliæ p'mate. W. Wynton Epo Cancellar' nro.
J.Roffen' Epo Thes' nostro. Ricardo Arundell. Thoma de Bello

campo, Warr' Roberto. Suff Comitibz. Waltero de Manny Guidone de brian. Johe de Grey de Retherfeld Senescallo hospicii nostri & aliis. Dat' p manu' nostra' apud Westmonasteriu' t'ciodecimo die Octobr Anno regni nostri Angliæ tricesimo secundo regni vero nostri franciæ decimo nono.

No. XI
Charter of Confirmation of King Richard II. A.D. 1385.

Ricardus dei g'cia Rex Angliæ &,franciæ & dominus hibinæ. Omnibz ad quos p'sentes Iræ puen'int salutem. Nos autem donaciones concessiones & confirmaciones p'dictas ratas hentes & gratas eas p'nobis & heredibz nostris quantu' in nobis e' acceptamus approbamus ratificamus & nunc Burgensibz villæ p'dcæ & eor' heredibz & successoribz Burgensibz villæ p'dcæ tenore p' senciu' concedim' & confirmamus sicut cartæ & Iræ patentes p'dcæ racionabiliter testantur & p' vt iidem Burgenses & eor' antecessores libertatibz & quietanciis p'dictis a tempore confeccionis Cartar' & Irar' p'dictar' racionabiliter vti & gaudere consueuerunt. In cui rei testimoniu' has Iras nostras fieri fecimus patentes. Teste me ipo apud Westmonasteriu duodecimo die Octobris. Anno regni nri octauo.

No. XII
Charter of Confirmation of King Edward IV. granted A. D.1463.

Edwardus dei g'cia Rex Angliæ domin' Hibniæ & dux Aquit' Archiepis Epis Abatibz Prioribz Comitibz Baronibz Justic' Vicecomitibz P'positis Ministris & omnibz Balliuis & fidelibz suis salutem. Nos autem donaciones cocessiones & confirmaciones p'dcas ratas hentes & g'tas eas p' nobis & heredibz nostris quantu' i nobis e' acceptamus approbamus ratificamus & nuc Burgensibz villæ p'dcae & eor' heredibz & successoribz Burgensibz villæ p'dcæ tenore presentiu' concedimus & confirmamus sicut cartæ & Iræ patentes p'dcæ racionabiliter testantur & p'vt iidem Burgenses * eoru' antecessores libertatibz et quietanciis p'dictis a tempore confeccionis cartar' & brar' p'dictaru' racionabiliter vti & gaudere consueuerunt. In cui' rei testimoniu' has Iras nostras fieri fecimus patentes. Teste me ipo apud Westmonasteriu' septimo die Februarii Anno regni nostri secundo

No. XIII
Charter of Confirmation granted by King *Richard* III.
Anno Domini, 1484.

Ricardus dei g'cia Rex Angliæ & Franciæ & dominus hibniæ. Omnibz ad quos p'sentes Iræ puen' int salutem. Nos autem dictas Iras de confirmacione libertatum franchesiar' quietanciaru' immunitatum ac alior' supradictoru' no' reuocatoru' de assensu & anisamento duoru' spualm & temporaliu' ac Commitat' regni, nostri. Angliæ in parliamento nostro nup apud Westmonasteri' celebrato existen' approbamus ratificamus & confirmamus p' vt Iræ p'dcæ racionabilit' testantur &p' vt iidem homines libertatibz franchesiis quietanciis & immunitatibz p'dictis vti debent ipi quæ & eoru' antecessores Burgenses p'dcæ *villæ* de *Portesmuth* libertatibz franchesiis quietanciis & immunitatibz illis a tempore confeccionis Irar p'dictaru' semp hactenus racionabiliter vti & gandere consueuerunt. In cuius rei testimoniu has ras nostras fieri fecimus patentes. Teste me ipo apud Westmonasteriu' quintodecimo die Junii: Anno regni nostri primo.

No. XIV.
Deed relating to the *Hospital* of *God's House* on the *Parade*.

Universis sanctæ matris ecclesiæ filiis Magister *Alanus de Stokes* officialis domini petri Winton episcopi salutem in domino. Noverint universi quod omnis controversia mota coram quibuscunque Judicibus inter priorem et conventum de *Suwicke* ex una parte et magistrum et fratres hospital domus dei de *Portesmuth* ex altera super jure parochiali Ecclesiæ suæ de *Portesmuth* in hac forma coram nobis amicabiliter conquievit. Concesserunt dictus Prior et Conventus quod in prefato ospitali jure parochiali ecclesiæ suæ de *Portesmuth* divina celebrentur per duos sacerdotes tum adhibito Rectore hospital, si fuit sacerdos. Et si aliquis externus sacerdos ibidem veniens transfretandi vel prognationis causa velit ibidem celebrare bene ei licebit Et habeant duas campanas non excedentes quantitatem campanarum matricis ecclesiæ quæ pulsent ad matutinas et ad missas et ad vespas et pro defunctis, et novam brevem post pulsationem NoVÆ matricis ecclesiæ tui *parochianos* de *Portesmuth* non recipiant dicti fratres ad confessionum neC ad communionem corporis Christi,excepto quod si aliquis ratiat infirmum et petat specialiter confessionem abaliquo sacerdote de ospitali, requisito primum consensu sacerdotis parochialis, ei non deneget. Nec aliquem externum ad confessionem recipient *publicé* in quadragesima in fratres et sorores et familiam et infirmos ibidem jacentes et hospitatos. Verumptamen si aliquis externus petierit consilium ab aliquo sacerdote de ospitali licebit in *privatim* recipere. Preterea diebus dominicis et in præcipuis *octo* festivitatibus, scilicet, die Natalisdomini, Epiphaniæ, Purificationis, Annuntiationis beatæ Mariæ, Ascentionis, domini, Assumptionis, et Nativits beatæ mariæ et in festo omnium Sanctorum, prædicti fratres hospitali parochianos de *Portesmuth* non recipient. Si forte contingit quod aliqui de præfatis parochianis in prædictis festivitatibus vel diebus dominicis ad prænominatum ospitale. divina audituri venerint, admittantur et eorum oblatio, si qua pervenerit, bona fide et integre matrici ecclesiæ sub pœna inferius expressa restituatur,ni hiidem parochiani praefatæ matrici ecclesiæ prædictis diebus satisfacerint. Propterea non licebit alicui de hospitali naves intrare, vel benedictionem faciat, vel prædicationem vel Evangelium legat seu elemosinam licite petat, lecto Eyangelio et facta sollempnitate per capellam matricis ecclesiæ. Concesserunt insuper dicti canonici quod hospitale habeat cimiterium fratribus turn et sororibus ejusdem hospitali,et familiis et pauperibus et aliis in eodem hospitali decedentibus, fratres autem et sorores in hoc scripto accipimus, eos, qui ibidem *habitum* susceperunt et deferunt vel si et sua eidem hospitali dederunt. Propterea si aliquis externus apud hospitale sepulturam elegerit, licebit eis libere eum recipere, si corpus primum deferetur ad matricem ecclesiam et *ibidem* missa celebrabitur. . Et sciendum quod *primum* legatum oportet *parochianosi* de *portesmuth* relinquiere matrici ecclesiæ, et sacerdos parochialis testamento *parochianorum* tenetur integrum pro dampnis, non quæ matrix ecclesiæ pro hac concessione sustinebit; solvent dicti fratres hospitali singulis annis *inperpetuum* matrici ecclesiæ *viginti solidos* sterlingorum ad quatuor terminos anni, scilicet in festo sancti Michælis v solidos, in circumcisione domini v solidos, ad pascham v solidos et in festo sancti Johannis Baptists v solidos; ad majorem vero securitatem dicti fratres mediante sacramento corporaliter præstito, tactis sacrosanctis, sub pœna stipulatione se obligaverunt, videlicet xl solidorum solvendorum memoratis Priori et Conventui si forte pœna fuit commissa, quod si post delictum canonicæ commoniti per viii dies non satisfecerint, pœna commissa sine contradictipne dictis Priori et Conventui solvatur. Quod omnibus ex parte Prioris et Conventus debet intelligi, facta est autem hæc compositio anno *primo*[133] post decessum *Stephani* de *langeton* tunc *Cantuariæ* Archiepiscopi. Et in hujus rei testimonium partes præsentem compositionem sigillis suis roboraverunt. Et nos quia dominus episcopus Winton absens fuit eam auctoritate ejusdem episcopi confirmavimus et signum nostrum appendimus, una cum signo magistri B. Archis' ejusdem loci. Hiis testibus Magistro A. de Eblesburn, magistro R. canonico, magistro J de Walingford, R. Decano Winton. W. Capellano Offic.. et multis aliis.

(Ex antiquo libro MS. in possessione Reverendi C.B. Henville, Vicarii de Portsmouth.)

NO. XV
The Will of *Thomas Eynolf*, of *Portsmouth*.[134]

Hoc est testamentu *Thomæ Eynolf* de *Portesmue*. Primo legat deo anima' sua' & corpus suu' t'rae ad sepeliendu' in cemiterio beati *Thomæ de Portesmue*. Ite ad *altare* bi *Thomæ Martiris* iiii. d'. Ite' fabrice ecce bi Thomæ inppetuu' vj d' recipiend' ad festu' sci michael' de vna domo quæ est ab oposito domu' *Aliciæ de murie-filde*. It' legat fratri Radulf' canonico vj d. It' fri Math' canonico iiii d'. It' dno Pet' capello iiii d'. It' legat duobz clericis iiii. d'. It' legat ecce bæ *mariæ* de *Suwyka* et canonicis ibm deo s'uientibz inppetu' vj d' annu' reddit' vt celebrant diuina in die obitus sui pcipiend illos vj denar' in die obitus

___

133 A.D. 1229

134 This MS. is in the same hand-writing as the preceding *deed* , and therefore evidently made about the same period.

sui de domo quam Brien aliquido tenuit. It' legat Walt Eynolf fratr' suo vna' tunica' & vnu' herigadm & vnu' sapiom de blueto & eciam vna' suptunicam de Russeto. It' legat Nich' filio p'dci Walt' vna suptunica' de blueto. It' legat Willo filio Walt' vj d'. It' legat Isabellæ filise p'dci Walt' xij d'. It' legat Julianæ soror' dcæ Isabellæ xij d. It' legat Johæ vxor' suæ solariu' cu' celariis & domibz cu' ptinenciis in latitudine & longitudine sicut postes in occidentali pte ostii condonat' omnibz diebz vitæ suæ & post decessu' vxor' revertet dcm solarium cu' domibz adjacentibz Willo Eynolf filio p'dci Thomæ, ita vt p'dcs Wills faciet inppetuu' celebrare Annuatim vna' missam in die obit' sui & dabit p'aia sua in die obit' sui annuati' inppetuu' yjd' in pane & quicuqz solariu' p'. tempore tenuerit, Et alia pars domus a postes vendat' ad debita soluenda & quod remanet media pars t'dat' Johæ vxor' suæ & altera pars exsecutoribz suis & dist' buat' p' aia sua. It' legat Johaæ vxor' suæ vna' domu' qm Brien tenuit inppetuu' sicut domus se extendet reddendo inde annuati' dno Regi ad festum sci michael' vj d' & P'ori & conuent' de *Sutwyk* vjd' in die obit' sui. It legat Pet'ouille filiæ suæ vna' culcitm.de plumet' & vna' arca'.quæ fuit Mat' suæ & vnu' tapetu' & duo linciamina integ'. It' legat Willo Eynolf filio suo medietate' vniu' *crofte* ab oposito *Aule Regis* in pte aq'lonar' saluo Johæ vxor' suæ domu' cu' alta pte & porta' quoad iuxerit reddendo inde Annuatim p'dcto Willo vjd' & p'dcs Wills aq'etavit p'dcam Joh' & tota' t'ram & post decessu' p'dcæ Johæ dca dom' & placia & porta reu' tet p'dco Willo. It' legat oia utencilia mobilia & immobilia in duas ptes, vna p-s.legat Johæ vxor' suæ & alt'ra pars vendat' & distr' buat' p' aia sua. It' legat Johæ vxori suæ.vnu' plubu' ita vt post decessu' p'dci' Thomæ redd' p'dca Johae xijd' ad 'clocherm sci Thom' mart'. It' legat Johæ vxor' suæ, meliore' truncu' de omnibz truncis & Annirectæ filiæ Willi Aynolf scdm meliore' truncu' It' legat Pho aynolf yj'd It' legat omnibz filiol' suis vn'cuisqz jd' It' legat" filiæ gimnildæ, xiiid qd p'dca .gimnilda m' debz. It']egat ad illuminare beatæ mariæ in ecclia bi Thomæ de *Portesmue* inppetuu' j.d' annu' reddit' pcipiend' Annuati.inppetuu' ad festu' sci michal' de Robto Damel. It' legat pet'uille filiæ suæ vna' domu' & placiam sicut domus se extendit except' placia vacua juxta ab oposito domu' Aliciæ de Muriefelde reddendo inde Annuatim inppetuu' eccæ Thom' mart' vjd' ad festu' sci michael' It' legat Johæ vxor' suæ vna' helna' t'ræ cu' blado astante quæ helua iacet in la *soneledelonde* int' t'ram Raginaldi le Wite & t'ram Steph' p'cbe & extendit, v'sus aq'lon' & austru' & post decessu' vxor' reuertet p'dca helua ad'Petrouillam. Et super hoc constituit exsecutor' suos Vnm Radulf' canonicu' de Sutwyk. Walter' Eynolf, Henr' de grangia. Thom' clerico.

Ibid.

No. XVI

Deed between the *Prior* of Southwick and the *Vicar* of *Portsmouth* relative to the *tithes* of the Town; A. D.1260.

Omnibus Christi fidelibus presentes literæ inspecturæ vel andituræ Magister *Thomas* de Winton. Official Winton Salutem in Domino sempiternam. Inter Religiosos yiros Priorem et Conventum de *Suthewyk* patronos Capellæ de Portesmuth et Rectores ex parte una et *Thomam de Sengelton* dictæ capellæ perpetuum *Vicarium* ex altera in hunc modum de unanimi assensu duximus ordinandum videlicet quod prædictus vicarius omnes oblaciones et obvenciones ad dictam capellam qualiscunque cum mortuariis et legatis ad ipsam spectantibus pertinentes et obvenientes linorum et canaborum necnon et minutas decimas de *villa* de *Portesmuth* pervenientes et omnia alia prout omnis predecessor vicarius percipere consuevit plenarie percipiat propter, decimas cujuslibet generis bladi solvendo annuatim ad quatuor terminos anni subscriptos Priori et Conventui

de *Suthewyk* pensionem *centum solidorum* legatium sterlingorum
videlicet ad festum omnium Sanctorum xx solidos ad festum
Purificationis beatæ Virginis xx solidos ad festum paschatis xl solidos
& ad festum Assumptions beatæ Virginis xx solidos. Et cum dicti
Prior et Conventus defectum librorum et ornamentorum dictæ
capellæ in statum debitum suffiicienter repariunt dictus yicarius cum
omnibus oneribus dictam Capellam contingentibus tam in serviciis
quam aliis ordinariis et extraordinariis prædictum in statu debito
sustinebit et consimiliter omnes Vicarii successores, qui pro tempore
fuerint in eadem vicaria inperpetuum prædicta augnoscent
obseruabunt et sustinebunt, habebit et dictus viearius *mansum*
canonicorum. in *Villa* de *Portesmuth* et successores sui vicarii ad
inhabitandum, excepta quadam aera ex parte boriali dicti mansi
muro interclusa, dictis Priori et Conventui reservata. Et ut hac
ordinatio de communi consensu publicum facta, stabilita, firmata et
inconcussa inperpetuum ipsam una nobiscum in modum Cirograffi
bipartitam Sigillorum suorum appositione alternatim facta
confirmaverunt et reboraverunt. Actum in Anno Domini M° CC• et
sexagesimo, terio die Maii.

Ibid.

No. XVII

Copies of two Certificates of Discharge for the *Abbot* of
Glastonbury.

Johan Hacket leutenant le conte *Arundel* pour la garde de
Portesmuth & conestable de *Porchestre* as vescontes de *Wiltshire* &
Barckshire, & a tous autres que cestes lettres verront ou orront sal.
en Dieu. Voillets scavoir le service l' Abbe de Glastingburgh etre bien
et suffiisament fait par tout le temps qu'ils besogne de morer pour la

dite garde, pour toutes ses terres en les dites contees, tanqu'a a la
date de cestes. En temoyance de queux choses aux cettes lettres
ouvertes jay mis mon seal. Escriptes a *Porcestre* le Lundy prochein
apres la circumcision. L'an du regne du Roy Edward Tierce apres la
Conqueste, doziemè.

Richard conte de *Arundel* assigne par nostre seignr. le Roy pour
la garde de la mer en *Hampshire*, as vescontes & autres ministres
nostre dit seignr. le Roy en la conte de *Wiltshire* & *Barckshire* sal.
pour ceo que *Johan Abbe de Glastenburgh* fait trouve plainement et
suffisament gents d'armes pour la garde de la mer en *Hampshire* a
Porcestre pour toutes les tems qu'ils tient en les avant dites contees
de *Wiltshire* & *Barchshire* selon ce que ces predecesseurs en temps
de necessite solent faire. Si com me par temonyance vous mandons
que au dit *Abbe*, ne a ses tenants bondes par resonde la dite garde, ne
face mal ne moleste tranqu' comme il continue la
dite garde en la maniere comme il fait, c'est a scavoir pour ses terres
en *Wiltshire* treys hommes d'armes & pour ses terres en *Barkshire*
un homme d'arme, &c. En temonyance de quelle chose a cette lettre
patente avons mys nostre seal. Donnè, a nostre *chastel* de *Arundel* 9
Mart l'an du Regne le Roy Edward le tierce apres la conqueste
troisiemè.

Ex Registro Abbatiæ Glaston. in Bibliotheca Dni Vicecom.
Weymouth. Fol. 128. 129.

ADDENDA

Since this work has gone to press, the Editor has been obligingly favoured with the following particulars respecting the Charter of Charles II by Mr. Palmer, of the Rolls Chapel Office, London:

The Charter of Charles the Second recites the surrender of former letters patent granted to the Corporation by King Charles the First. — Incorporates the Borough of Portsmouth, and the *Town of Gosport* a *Free Borough*, by the name of the Mayor, Aldermen and Burgesses of the Borough of Portesmouth, in the county of Southampton. —Grants that one of the more honest and discreet Aldermen shall be elected Mayor; that twelve of the Burgesses of the said Borough shall be elected Aldermen for *life*, besides the Mayor for the time being; that the said Aldermen shall be the council of the said Borough, and aiding and assisting to the Mayor; that the Mayor, Recorder, and Aldermen, and their Successors, or the major part of them (of whom the Mayor and Recorder to be always two) shall have full power to appoint bye laws, and impose such reasonable fines, &c. upon all delinquents against such laws. —Appoints *Thomas Hancock* to be the first *Mayor*, and James Duke of York and others to be the first Burgesses. Power to impose a fine of £10 upon any one refusing to undertake the office of Mayor or Aldermen. Licence to the Mayor (in case of sickness or absence) to appoint a deputy. Appoints *Sir John Biggs* to be the first *Recorder;* power in the Mayor and Aldermen to *appoint in the room of Sir John Biggs another Recorder. The Mayor to be Clerk of the Market. The Charter reserves the power of removing the Mayor, Aldermen, &c at the WILL AND PLEASURE of his MAJESTY. That the Mayor, &c and their Successors, may hold and keep a fair or mart, in every year, for ever, to begin ad festum sancti Petri ad Vincula* to continue the whole of that day and for *fourteen* days next immediately following, according to letters patent of King Richard the Second, granted to the *Men of Portsmouth*, the said Mayor, &c. to relinquish the holding of a certain *fair* which was accustomed to be held on the *first* of August. And further the said Charter grants and confirms to the said Mayor, Aldermen, and Burgesses, the free passage by water from Portsmouth to Gosport, and from Portsmouth to Ryde, in the Isle of Wight, and the liberty of having and maintaining boats, &c. for the purpose of transporting to and fro persons with their goods and merchandize.

ACCOUNT
OF
POSTS, STAGE COACHES, WAGGONS, PACKETS, WATERMEN'S FARES, &c.

POSTS.

The general Post-office is situated at the upper end of St. Thomas's-street; the Naval Post-office, as well for the delivery as receipt of Merchants' and King's Ships, Letters, is near the lower end of Broad-street on the Point, there are likewise Offices for receiving letters in Queen-street, Portsea; at the Halfway-houses, and at the Bush Inn, Southsea. The letters are delivered in Portsmouth, Portsea, and the environs, soon after nine o'clock in the morning.

COACHES.

The London Mail sets out every evening from the Crown Inn, at half-past seven o'clock, and stops at the Angel, St. Clements.

Neyler's Post-coach, the Hero, sets out every morning at eight o'clock, from the Crown Inn, High-street, to the Golden Cross, Charing Cross, and Spread Eagle, Gracechurch-street.

The Lord Nelson, Post-coach, sets out every evening at seven o'clock from the Blue Posts Inn, Point, and stops at the Spread Eagle, in Gracechurch-street, and the Golden Cross, Charing Cross.

Cross and Co.'s Light Coach, the Rocket, sets out every morning at nine o'clock from the Fountain Inn, and stops at the White Bear, Piccadilly, and Belle Sauvage, Ludgate Hill.

Billett's Light Coach, the Princess Charlotte, sets out from the George Inn, High-street; No. 28, Broad-street, Point; 66, St. George's-square; 8, on the Hard; and the Royal Oak, Queen-street, Portsea, every morning at eight o'clock, and stops at the Angel Inn,

St. Clements; Bolt in Tun, Fleet-street; and George and Gate, Grace-church street.

The Wellington Light Coach sets out from the King of Prussia's, on the Point, three times every week, and stops at the Bull and Mouth Inn.

A Bristol Mail every night at five o'clock.

A Coach to Plymouth every Tuesday, Thursday, and Saturday morning, at eight o'clock.

A Coach to Chichester every morning at half-past eight o'clock.

WAGGONS

Clark's London Waggon, sets out from the Blue Posts Inn, Point, and No. 5, on the Hard, Portsea, every morning at eleven o'clock, and puts up at the White Hart and Ship Inn, in the Borough.

Pescott's (late Whitlow's) London Waggons, set out daily from No. 46, Broad-street, Point, and No. 112 Queen-street, Portsea, and put up at the Bell Inn, Wood-street, Cheapside, the King's Head, and Nag's Head Inns, in the Borough.

Sayer's light Fly Waggon, sets out three times a week from the Globe Inn, Oyster-street, and the Fountain Inn, High-street, and puts up at the Talbot Inn, in the Borough, and the Saracen's Head, Friday-street, Cheapside.

Cross and Co.'s Light Waggons, set out every day from the Fountain Inn, and put up at the Talbot Inn, Borough, and the Saracen's Head, Friday-street, Cheapside.

Salisbury, Bath, and Bristol Waggons, set out twice a week-from the Globe Inn, Oyster-street.

PACKETS.

The Wellbank, and Thomas and Elizabeth Packets, sail every Thursday and Friday, from the Quebec Tavern, Bath Square, Point, to Havre de Grace.

A Packet sails to Ryde, every morning at nine o'clock, and afternoon at three o'clock, from the Quebec Tavern, Point.

A Packet to Cowes every afternoon at half-past two o'clock, from the King's Head, Point.

A Packet to Lymington, three times a week, from the Thatched House, Point.

The Southampton Hoy sails from the White Hart, Point, on Tuesdays, Thursdays, and Saturdays. —The time of sailing depends on the tide.

To Plymouth and Torbay, three times a week from the Neptune and Mars, Point.

To Poole, Horsman's vessel sails from the King's Head, Point, every Friday; and Manlaw's vessel on every Tuesday, Thursday, and Saturday, from the Roebuck, Point.

To Guernsey, once a week, from the True Blue, on the Point.

Boats go every day to Porchester, but the time depends on the tide.

WATERMEN'S FARES.

Rates and Fares to be paid to Watermen limited and assessed by the commissioners appointed under the Gosport Portsmouth, and Portsea Ferry Act; to commence on the first of May, 1816.

FINE WEATHER FARES,
TO AND FROM
GOSPORT, PORTSMOUTH, AND PORTSEA.

	s	d
Every passenger, and not exceeding six, each	0	1
For the hire of a wherry, for one passenger, and not exceeding four	0	8
For five, and not exceeding six	1	0

FOUL WEATHER FARES.

	s	d
Every passenger, and not exceeding six, each	0	3
For the hire of a wherry, for one passenger, and not exceeding four	1	0
For five, and not exceeding six	1	0

FINE WEATHER FARES

To be increased *one half* when the Blue Flag is hoisted; and *doubled* in foul weather, when the red Triangular Flag is hoisted

	s	d
For the hire of a wherry to Forton Mill	1	6
To Weovil or Weovil Common	1	0

To Hardway	1	0
For more than four, and not exceeding eight, each	0	3
For returning with the same party from the above place	0	6
To Wicker's Hard, for one passenger; and not exceeding four	2	6
For more than four, and not exceeding eight	3	6
For returning with the same party	1	0
To Fareham, for one passenger, and not exceeding four	3	6
For more than four, and not exceeding eight	4	6
For returning with the same party	1	0
To Porchester for one passenger, and not exceeding four	2	6
For more than four, and not exceeding eight	3	6
For returning with the same party	1	0
To Paulsgrove for one passenger, and not exceeding four	3	6
For more than four, and not exceeding-eight	4	6
For returning with the same party	1	0
Other passengers returning, each	0	6
To Haslar Hospital	0	9
To Stoke	2	0
To Fareham Lake, above Hardway	2	0

To Porchester Lake	1	6
For returning with the same party from either of the above places	0	6
Other passengers returning, each	0	3
From Portsmouth or Portsea, to Cold Harbour, Gosport	0	9
To Blockhouse Point	0	6
To the Bathing Machines at Southsea Common	1	0
To Southsea Castle	1	6
To Haslar Barracks, for one passenger, and not exceeding four	1	6
For five, and not exceeding eight	2	6
For returning with the same party	0	6
To Ryde, Nettlestone, or Priory, for one passenger, and not exceeding four	5	0
For returning with the same party	1	6
For five, and not exceeding eight	6	0
For returning with the same party	1	6
To Fish House, for one passenger, and not exceeding four	5	6
For returning with the same party	1	0
For five, and not exceeding eight	6	6
For returning with the same party	1	6

To Wotton Bridge for one passenger, and not exceeding four	6	0
For returning with the same party	1	0
For five, and not exceeding eight	7	6
For returning with the same party	1	6
To Brading	8	0
For returning with the same party	1	6
To Stoke's bay, for one passenger, and not exceeding four	3	6
For returning with the game party	1	0
To Spithead, for one passenger, and not exceeding four	3	0
For returning with the same party	1	0
For five, and not exceeding eight	4	0
For returning with the same party	1	0
To more ships.than one, each ship	0	6
For every passenger taken in at Spithead, not exceeding eight, each	0	6
To Cowes, for any number not exceeding eight	8	0
For returning with the same party	2	0

FREIGHT FOR CATTLE

	s	d
Horses, Mules, and Bullocks, in horse boats, each	2	0
Calves, Sheep, and Hogs, in wherries or other boats, each	0	3

FREIGHT FOR GOODS.

	s	d
A wherry to St. Helen's to take cases, bales, trunks, or other articles, not exceeding 8 cwt.	7	0
To Spithead, not exceeding 8cwt.	3	0
To the Motherbank, not exceeding 8 cwt.	5	0
To Cowes	8	0
To Stokes Bay	4	0
To all vessels lying in the Harbour Channel, not exceeding 8 cwt.	2	0

And an additional charge of 3d, on every other cwt not to exceed 16 cwt on each of the above fares.

Two square of light goods to be considered as equal to 1cwt.

¶The Flag to denote dangerous weather is a *Broad Pendant, blue and red.* No waterman is compelled to work on the passage, during the time this flag is hoisted.

THE DISTANCES OF ROADS FROM PORTSMOUTH
TO MANY OF
THE PRINCIPAL TOWNS
IN
ENGLAND

TO LONDON

	Miles.		Miles.
Petersfield	18	Kingston	11
Liphook	8	*London*	11
Godalming	12		—
Ripiey	12	Total	72

TO OXFORD

	Miles.		Miles.
Southwick	8	Aldermaston	9
Wickham	4	Pangbourn	6
Waltham	5	Wallingford	10½
Titchbourn	8½	*Oxford*	12¼
Alresford	2¼		—
Dummer	9	Total	78½
Worting	4		

TO SALISBURY

	Miles.		Miles.
Wickham	11¾	Aldermaston	9
Botley		White Parish	1
Mensbridge		Whaddon	3½
Stoneham	16¾	Alderbury	¾
Rumsey		*Salisbury*	3¼
Heath Post	2¼		—
Dummer	6	Total	45½

TO ARUNDEL

	Miles.		Miles.
Havant	9	Croker Hill	2
Emsworth	2	Mackrel's Bridge	2¼
Nutbourn	1½	Almsford Hill	¾
Fishbourn	3½	*Arundel*	3
Chichester	2		—
Maudling	2	Total	28

TO BRIGHTHELMSTONE

	Miles.		Miles.
Arundel, as before	28	The Pad	1
Angmering Park	4	Shoreham Bridge	¼
Patching Pond	1	*Brighthelmstone*	7 ¼
Sompting	5		
Lanceing	1		—
		Total	48

TO SOUTHAMPTON

	Miles.		Miles.
Fareham	8	*Southampton*	7
Botley	8	Total	23

ANOTHER ROAD BY PORTSDOWN

	Miles.		Miles.
Portsdown	6	*Southampton*	7
Wickham	6		—
Botley	4	Total	23
Sompting	5		
Lanceing	1		

ANOTHER ROAD OVER NORTHAM AND BURLESDON BRIDGES

	Miles.		Miles.
Fareham	9	*Southampton*	5
Titchfiled	2		—
Burlesdon	5	Total	21

TO CHICHESTER

			Miles.
Cosham	4½	*Chichester*	2
Havant	4½		—
Nutbourn	3½	Total	18
Fishbourn	3½		

TO YARMOUTH

			Miles.
Cowes	14	*Yarmouth*	6½
Newton	7		—
		Total	27½

TO WINCHESTER

			Miles.
Southwick	7¼	*Winchester*	10
Wickham	4		—
Waltham	5¼	Total	27

TO ROMSEY

			Miles.
Cosham	4¼	Winchester	10
Fareham	4¾	*Romsey*	11
Wickham	4		—
Waltham	5¼	Total	27

TO STOCKBRIDGE

			Miles.
Southwick	7¾	*Stockbridge*	8 ½
Wickham	4		
Waltham	5¼	Total	35 ½
Winchester	10		

FINIS

216